KU-545-635

Essential
Lanzarote
& Fuerteventura

by Andrew Sanger

Andrew Sanger is a well-established travel
journalist who has contributed to a wide
range of popular magazines and most British
newspapers. He is the author of more than a
dozen travel guides, including *Essential
Tenerife* and *Explorer Israel* for the AA. He has
twice won at the annual Travelex Travel
Writers' Awards.

Above: *Playa de Papagayo, Lanzarote*

AA Publishing

Above: *lace-making at Bodega Santa Maria*

Front cover: *El Golfo; windsurfers at Teguise; girl in traditional costume*
Back cover: *Malvasia wine barrels*

Written by Andrew Sanger
Updated by Paul Murphy

Published and distributed in the United Kingdom by AA Publishing, a trading name of Automobile Association Developments Limited, whose registered office is Norfolk House, Priestley Road, Basingstoke, Hampshire, RG24 9NY. Registered number 1878835.

© Automobile Association Developments Limited 2001
Maps © Automobile Association Developments Limited 2001
Reprinted 2001. Information verified and updated.

Automobile Association Developments Limited retains the copyright in the original edition © 1999 and in all subsequent editions, reprints and amendments.

A CIP catalogue record for this book is available from the British Library.

ISBN 0 7495 1917 7

The contents of this publication are believed correct at the time of printing. Nevertheless, the publishers cannot be held responsible for any errors or omissions or for changes in the details given in this guide or for the consequences of any reliance on the information it provides. Assessments of attractions, hotels, restaurants and other sights are based upon the author's personal experience and, therefore, necessarily contain elements of subjective opinion which may not reflect the publisher's opinion or dictate a reader's own experience on another occasion.

We have tried to ensure accuracy in this guide, but things do change and we would be grateful if readers would advise us of any inaccuracies they may encounter.

Find out more about AA Publishing and the wide range of services the AA provides by visiting our web site at www.theAA.com

Colour separation: Pace Colour, Southampton
Printed and bound in Italy by Printer Trento S.r.l.

Contents

About this Book

KEY TO SYMBOLS

✚ map reference to the maps found in the What to See section

✉ address or location

☎ telephone number

🕐 opening times

🍴 restaurant or café on premises or near by

Ⓜ nearest underground train station

🚌 nearest bus/tram route

🚇 nearest overground train station

🚢 ferry crossings and boat excursions

✈ travel by air

ℹ tourist information

♿ facilities for visitors with disabilities

✋ admission charge

↔ other places of interest near by

❓ other practical information

▶ indicates the page where you will find a fuller description

Essential *Lanzarote & Fuerteventura* is divided into five sections to cover the most important aspects of your visit to the islands.

Viewing Lanzarote & Fuerteventura
pages 5–14
An introduction to the islands by the author.
Features of Lanzarote & Fuerteventura
Essence of Lanzarote & Fuerteventura
The Shaping of Lanzarote & Fuerteventura
Peace and Quiet
Famous of Lanzarote & Fuerteventura

Top Ten pages 15–26
The author's choice of the Top Ten places to see on the islands, listed in alphabetical order, each with practical information.

What to See pages 27–90
The islands of Lanzarote & Fuerteventura, each with its own brief introduction and an alphabetical listing of the main attractions.
Practical information
Snippets of 'Did you know...' information
4 suggested walks
4 suggested tours
3 features

Where To... pages 91–116
Detailed listings of the best places to eat, stay, shop, take the children and be entertained.

Practical Matters pages 117–24
A highly visual section containing essential travel information.

Maps
All map references are to the individual maps found in the What to See section of this guide.
For example, Islote de Hilario has the reference ✚ 28B2 – indicating the page on which the map is located and the grid square in which the mountain is to be found. A list of the maps that have been used in this travel guide can be found in the index.

Prices
Where appropriate, an indication of the cost of an establishment is given by **£** signs:

£££ denotes higher prices, **££** denotes average prices, while **£** denotes lower charges.

Star Ratings
Most of the places described in this book have been given a separate rating:

✿✿✿ Do not miss
✿✿ Highly recommended
✿ Worth seeing

Viewing
Lanzarote
& Fuerteventura

Above: Fuerteventura is a world centre for windsurfing
Right: basket-weaving in Fuerteventura

5

Andrew Sanger's Lanzarote & Fuerteventura

A Long Way From Spain

Though Spanish, Lanzarote and Fuerteventura are much nearer to the Sahara than to Spain. These two most easterly of the Canary Islands are only around 96km from the coast of Africa. Lanzarote is the most northerly of the Canaries. Lanzarote and Fuerteventura possess four smaller isles; Lobos, La Graciosa, Alegranza and Montaña Clara.

There's something in the harsh paradox of these volcanic islands that thrills the soul. The austere, timeless emptiness; the dryness recalling the nearby Sahara; the menacing hint of nature's enduring power, the overwhelming solitude and silence – all these beckon, yet defy man to make a home here.

These islands are indeed very thinly populated. Fuerteventura's average of 11 people per square kilometre is the lowest in the Canaries, and even that figure gives no clue to the sense of space, for almost everyone lives in just one place – Puerto del Rosario. Lanzarote's case, while not quite as extreme, is similar: most people live in Arrecife.

Yet these are not desert islands, but Spanish territories with agriculture, art, history, traditions and folkore, culture and cuisine. They are also holiday lands with hotels, beaches, satellite TV and hire cars.

That is the paradox. The destructive forces of nature – exemplified by the eruption of Timanfaya volcano in the 1730s, when burning rock rained on Lanzarote and swept away fields and villages that islanders had nurtured for centuries – have themselves now been harnessed by man's own great powers of survival and imagination. Getting visitors to pay to see the volcanoes, and using the heat of the Fire Mountains to barbecue steaks, is a victory of sorts. A temporary one, perhaps, for the volcanoes may erupt again one day, and the sands continue to blow over from Africa.

The enticing main beach of Puerto del Carmen, Lanzarote

Features of Lanzarote & Fuerteventura

People

• Some 54,000 people live on Lanzarote and about 30,000 on Fuerteventura. On both islands, over half the population live in their respective capital.

• Ethnically the islanders are thought to be a mix of Berber, Arab, Norman and Spanish.

• Fuerteventura natives are known as *maioreros*, while Lanzaroteños are called *conejos*, meaning rabbits.

A Tropical Wind

Nearly all of Lanzarote and Fuerteventura's holiday accommodation is on south-facing coasts, which are sheltered from the prevailing trade winds (*alisios*, in Spanish). Trade winds, found only in tropical regions, blow form the northwest. Lying between the 28th and 29th parallels, Lanzarote and Fuerteventura are less than 645km from the Tropic of Cancer.

Left: a Lanzaroteño takes time to reflect

Climate

• Unlike the other Canaries, these two islands remain practically rainfree all year round, though there can be winter cloud. Any rain that does fall normally comes between December and February, and falls on an average of only 16 days per year, with a total annual precipitation of only about 138mm.

• Average daytime temperatures remain almost constant at around 20°C on Lanzarote, 19°C on Fuerteventura all year round.

• Both islands can be windy, especially on the western sides.

Size

• The second largest of the Canaries, Fuerteventura is only slightly smaller than Tenerife. At 1,731sq km, it is over twice the size of Lanzarote's 813sq km.

Language

• Spanish is the language of the Canaries, but islanders also have a patois of their own. English is widely spoken (though not usually very well), especially at resorts and tourist attractions.

Right: Lanzarote still blooms despite the lack of rain

Essence of Lanzarote & Fuerteventura

Awesome dunes run along the coast of northeast Fuerteventura

Most people visiting these two most easterly of the Canary Islands are looking for sun, sea, sand and sights; but look too for earth, wind and fire. Over the millennia, these powerful natural forces have given Lanzarote and Fuerteventura their distinctive character: dramatic volcanic landscapes, waterless – but not barren – hills, and gorgeous beaches of pure Sahara sand are the impressive legacy.

These islands have avoided the overdevelopment and 'lager lout' culture of many other popular sunshine destinations. Low-key family resorts, well-equipped small complexes, inland villas with pools, and an unspoiled blue and gold coastline give Lanzarote and Fuerteventura a civilised air.

THE **10** ESSENTIALS

If you only have a short time to visit Lanzarote and Fuerteventura, or would like to get a complete picture of the islands, here are the essentials:

• **See twigs burst into flame** on Islote de Hilario. The scorching ground temperature ignites brushwood and boils water in seconds (➤ 20–1).

• **Take the bus tour** from Islote de Hilario. It's the only way to get into the very heart of volcano country.

• **Visit the Fundación César Manrique**. The genius and flair of the man who made Lanzarote great can be felt in his former home (➤ 19), which is now an important art gallery.

• **Go to the Jameos del Agua** during the day just to gaze and wonder, or in the evening for a night out in an amazing setting (➤ 22).

• **Eat** *papas arrugadas con mojo*. These ultra-tasty, salty new potatoes are one of the best local specialities (➤ 82–3). *Mojo* is a traditional Canarian piquant sauce.

• **Drink Lanzarote wine**. If you think a barren volcanic landscape is not the best place to grow grapes, you haven't tried Lanzarote's cool, crisp and dry Malvasia white wines.

• **Sunbathe on a golden beach**, not the grainy black stuff more typical of the other Canaries. Lanzarote and Fuerteventura have long, wide stretches of fine pale sands.

• **Walk ten paces on the** *malpaís*. To understand just how unworkable this land is, try walking on it. The best place to try this is La Geria (➤ 26), where it's easy to pull over to the side of the road and get out of the car.

• **Walk on giant sand dunes**. East of Lanzarote's Playa Blanca, or in Fuerteventura's Dunes Natural Park or Pared Isthmus, stroll on the rolling, drifting desert sandscapes.

• **Take a trip to another island**. Whether you're on Lanzarote or Fuerteventura, it's worth making a day trip to see the sights of the other. It's also fun to visit Isla Graciosa (off Lanzarote) or Isla de Lobos (off Fuerteventura).

Timanfaya's volcanic heat ignites brushwood in no time

Playa de Sotavento, Fuerteventura

The Shaping of Lanzarote & Fuerteventura

17–20 million years ago
Huge volcanic eruptions create Fuerteventura and Lanzarote.

2000–2500 BC
The islands are occupied by the Guanches, a tall, white race, thought to have been Berbers from north Africa; they speak a language recognisably related to that of the Berbers.

82 BC
Roman sailors visit the two eastern Canary Islands. Greek and Roman tradition refers to the Canaries as the Fortunate Isles.

CAD 1
Juba II of Mauretania

Jean de Béthencourt

sends an expedition to explore the Fortunate Isles. All the islands are then named, one of them being called Canaria on account of its wild dogs (Latin *canis*, dog).

CAD 1000
Arab raiders pay a first visit, taking a few Guanche slaves; they call the islands Kaledat.

1312
Genoese sailor Lancelotto Malocello visits Fuerteventura and Lanzarote (which is a corruption of his name).

1339
Mallorcan cartographer Angelino Dolcet draws the first map showing the Canaries, though he only includes Fuerteventura and Lanzarote.

1341
A Genoese expedition reports that Fuerteventura (and perhaps Lanzarote) is covered in goats and trees.

1350–1450
Assorted raiders and slavers pause at the islands to capture slaves.

1402
Two Normans, Gadifer de la Salle and Jean de Béthencourt, land on Lanzarote, basing themselves on the Rubicón coastline (west of Playa Blanca). They claim the islands for the king of Spain.

1405
Jean de Béthencourt and de la Salle establish a first settlement on Fuerteventura at Betancuria and begin the process of colonisation.

Early 1400s
Norman and Spanish settlers enslave the Guanches and build European-style farming villages.

1400–1500
French, English, Dutch and Arab pirates raid both islands, capturing both Guanche and mixed-blood slaves. Most are sold at Valencia, in Spain.

1730–6
Timanfaya eruptions destroy a third of Lanzarote. Many islanders flee to Europe and South America.

1824
New volcanic eruptions add to the destruction and the layer of *malpaís*.

1919
César Manrique is born in Arrecife, Lanzarote. As a young man he leaves to study art in Madrid.

1924
Don Miguel Unamuno is exiled to Fuerteventura, and praises its harsh simplicty.

1940s
Fascist Spain is believed to use southern Fuerteventura to assist Nazis.

Early 1960s
Package tourism to the Canaries begins.

1968
César Manrique returns to Lanzarote and completes his first major landscape work, Jameos del Agua. Timanfaya is set aside as a protected natural area, and limitations are placed on its development.

1970
Timanfaya begins to receive tourists, and Manrique opens El Diablo restaurant.

1970–7
The period of César Manrique's prolific landscape and conservation work on Lanzarote. Most of his great Lanzarote 'landscape and tourism' projects were completed at this time.

1974
The Spanish Government declares Timanfaya a National Park to be strictly protected.

A 300-year-old map of the Canary Islands

1978
Manrique receives the World Ecology and Tourism Award.

1986
Manrique receives the Europa Nostra Award for conservation work on Lanzarote.

1990
Jardín de Cactus, the last of Manrique's tourist attractions, is completed.

1992
César Manrique is killed in a car accident at the Tahíche junction, on 25 September.

1993
The Corralejo dunes on Fuerteventura are made a Natural Park. UNESCO declares the whole island of Lanzarote a world biosphere reserve.

11

Peace & Quiet

It's hard *not* to get away from it all on Lanzarote, while on Fuerteventura it's even easier to escape the crowd. The fledgeling tourist industry on both islands is confined to a small number of resorts, with huge areas of unspoiled countryside, dunes, beaches and volcanic *malpaís* all within a short distance.

Exploring

Use the road map from Lanzarote's tourist offices to find minor roads and tracks (some are in very poor condition) leading into the heart of deserted island scenery or down to empty beaches and bays. Or leave the crowd behind just by walking away along the long sandy beaches and rocky coasts.

Fuerteventura, too, is crossed by minor tracks and trails where neither tourists nor locals are much seen. With a four-wheel-drive, follow tracks on the Jandía Peninsula to beautiful, lonely sands. Beware, though, of swimming in such lonely places, especially on the west coast of Fuerteventura, as undercurrents can be dangerous.

Nature Reserves

Both islands have large protected zones where development has been forbidden, and where distinctive flora and fauna can be spotted. In fact, despite the seemingly barren landscape, Lanzarote and Fuerteventura are a haven for certain rare plants and birds and even harbour several native species unique to these two islands.

Lanzarote's offshore island, La Graciosa, though easily accessible by ferry from Orzola, is a place to find perfect solitude. The other, more remote islands, Montaña Clara and Alegranza, are breeding grounds for little shearwaters and Bulwer's petrels. In northern Lanzarote, the almost deserted sands of Famara beach are backed by rugged 700m cliffs, where Eleonora's falcons breed.

Lanzarote's cacti were cultivated for cochineal beetles to live on

On and below the cliffs, yellow-flowering *Pulicaria canariensis* fleabane, *Argyranthemum ochroleucum*, looking like an unkempt ragwort, and the pretty yellow daisy bush *Astericus schultzii* flourish: all are unique to Lanzarote and Fuerteventura. On the clifftop grows *Ferula lancerottensis*, the umbellifer also unique to this location. You'll see, too, attractive Canarian varieties of the euphorbia succulents, which positively thrive around the islands' coasts, such as the swollen-stemmed *Euphorbia canariensis*.

Inland, the Famara heights descend into the lush Haría valley, where a gentle micro-climate creates a miniature world of flourishing palms, cacti and several unique species of plant.

Did you know ?

Surprisingly, that well-known, bright yellow songbird called Serinus canaria *is not seen here. The Canaries are not named after the birds, as some believe, but the other way round. The islands were called after quite a different native – wild dogs (the Latin* canis *means dog), probably those found on Fuerteventura. A white-pawed local breed still survives, the descendant of the original inhabitants.*

Desertscapes

Fuerteventura's dry, barren, unpopulated landscapes and the tracts of sand dunes are just the place to find peace and quiet, and discover the low, clinging plants that can live here. The sandy Jandía Peninsula gives its name to the red-flowered cactus-like *Euphorbia handiensis* succulent, found only on these beaches. Climb the high slopes behind to find the straggling blue-flowering *Echium handiense* bugloss, also unique to this island.

On both islands, the houbara bustard, cream-coloured courser and black-bellied sandgrouse – rare species elsewhere – are at home in the dry, desert-like *malpais* and dunes. Several native birds seen here are paler versions of their European cousins, for example the rare Canarian chat, Berthelot's pipit and short-toed lark. You'll also see the trumpeter finch, with its short red beak, and hear its unmistakable call.

A lovely monarch butterfly spotted at the Agricultural Museum, Lanzarote

Spectacular views of the offshore islands to the north of Lanzarote

Famous of Lanzarote & Fuerteventura

Fundación César Manrique is housed in the artist's former home

César Manrique

César Manrique (1919–92) was born in Arrecife and made Lanzarote famous. The local lad, whose genius made him an international figure in the world of modern art, actually left Lanzarote as a young man. He prospered in New York, Paris and Madrid, formed close friendships with his compatriots Picasso and Miró, and became an acclaimed modern artist.

He eventually returned home in 1968 to a hero's welcome. Manrique adored the island, and was fascinated by man's relationship with landscape. He was also intrigued by the mass tourism then taking off in the Canaries – its destructive power, and equally, the benefits it could bring. Manrique was eager to ensure that development took place with respect for local culture and tradition.

The regional council gave him a free hand to do whatever he wanted, and Lanzarote became Manrique's *atelier*. He laid down autocratic architectural rules. He banned all roadside billboards (take a look, there aren't any). He put up fantastic, wind-driven giant mobile sculptures at major crossroads. He took over Lanzarote's geographical oddities and with sheer brilliance turned them into extraordinary attractions.

Many of his ideas became law, including the rules that no new buildings may be more than two storeys (except in Arrecife and tourist zones) high, and that window shutters must be plain wood or green, except by the sea, where blue is allowed. While new coastal developments disregard some rules, there are still no high-rise hotels.

In 1978 Manrique received the World Ecology and Tourism Award, and in 1986 the Europa Nostra Award for conservation. In 1992, at the age of 74, César Manrique died in a car crash at the intersection near his home (which he had said for years was dangerous). He is buried at Haría, and today is regarded by the islanders almost in the light of a secular saint.

Top Ten

Note: except for No 3, all the Top Ten sights are on Lanzarote

Above: *street lighting in Teguise*
Right: *a country islander takes a break*

1
Castillo de San José

An important collection of modern art is housed in this beautiful little semicircular stone fortress on a clifftop overlooking the sea.

✝ 29C2

✉ 3km north of Arrecife on Costa Teguise road

☎ 928 81 23 21

🕐 Daily 11–9

🍴 Restaurant (£££), bar (£)

🚌 Every 30 mins from Arrecife waterfront, every hour at weekends and festivals

ℹ 6 Avenida Gen Franco, Arrecife ☎ 928 81 18 60

♿ Few

✋ Free

↔ Castillo de San Gabriel (► 32)

Above: the 'Hunger Fortress' now houses an art gallery and an imaginative modern restaurant

The commanding position of San José Castle once made it a vital defence for the island's capital and port against the pirates who plagued the Canaries. Today it looks down on the busy commercial harbour of Puerto de Naos.

Built of black basalt in the midst of a period of great suffering after the eruption of Timanfaya, the castle came to be known as the Hunger Fortress. It is entered by crossing a moat, and the year of its completion, 1779, is carved above the entrance. Despite its strictly military purpose, the two-storey castle possesses great elegance and charm both inside and out. Its spacious halls and spiral stairwells, and the sharp contrast of black stone and white walls, create an atmosphere of powerful, stark simplicity. Floors are paved with patterned black volcanic slabs and black pebbles. The barrel-vaulted ceilings, too, are black.

In 1976 César Manrique restored the castle and installed the Museo Internacional de Arte Contemporáneo (International Museum of Contemporary Art) devoted to abstract modern art. The fantastic juxtaposition of vivid 20th-century forms and the black 18th-century fortress is startling, especially just inside the dark entrance, where a modern sculpture in glistening white marble stands. However, the paintings are poorly labelled and no catalogue is available.

Spiral steps lead down to César Manrique's own contribution, a glass-walled restaurant and bar overlooking the sea, with black tables, black napkins and modern classical music playing.

2

Cueva de los Verdes
(Greens' Cave)

The guided 2km walk through part of one of the longest lava cave systems in the world is enhanced by lighting, music and natural illusions.

Monte Corona is an extinct volcano in northern Lanzarote, whose eruptions some 5,000 years ago created a *malpaís* – a contorted, blackened landscape similar to Timanfaya at the other end of the island. The Corona eruptions formed one of the world's longest lava caves, Cueva de los Verdes and neighbouring Jameos del Agua being part of the same 7.5km Corona system (of which 1.5km is beneath the seabed). These hollow tubes were carved out as older basalt rock was melted and washed away by the lava flowing around it, and underground gases inflated the molten terrain.

The network of caverns and tunnels has long been known to locals, who used to hide here during the 17th century when Arab slave hunters and pirates raided the island. Cueva de los Verdes (not in fact a 'green' cave – Verde was the family name of former owners) is a short section reached by descending to a tunnel below ground level. Hour-long guided visits in English take visitors along a circular 2km walkway, narrow and low-ceilinged in places. Haunting music and lighting heighten the experience, which takes in vividly coloured rocks, a large hall called the Refuge, which can only be entered by one person at a time, impressive rock formations and a clever optical illusion at the end of the tour.

The entrance and ticket booth to the caves have been discreetly arranged to avoid disfiguring the barren seashore *malpaís*, which can be explored on footpaths.

29D4

Near Arrieta (26km north of Arrecife)

928 17 32 20

Daily 10–6 (last tour at 5)

Casa Miguel (£), Arrieta waterfront

No 9 passes about 1km away

6 Avenida Gen Franco, Arrecife 928 81 18 60

None (unsuitable for anyone who cannot walk and bend with ease)

Moderate

Los Jameos del Agua (► 22)

Amazing rock formations inside the volcanic caves

3

The Dunes of Fuerteventura

✚ 76C1, 77E5

🍴 Hotels Tres Islas and Oliva Beach have restaurants (££) and bars. Restaurants (£) in Corralejo. Also La Pared (£) and Costa Calma (£–££) at La Pared

🚌 No 6 (Corralejo–Puerto del Rosario)

🚢 To Corralejo from Playa Blanca on Lanzarote takes 40 minutes.

✈ Airport just south of the Parque Natural

ℹ Plaza Grande, Corralejo ☎ 928 86 62 35; the shopping centre, Morro Jable ☎ 928 54 07 76

↔ Corralejo (➤ 80), Isla de Lobos (➤ 84), La Oliva (➤ 88), Tarajalejo (➤ 89), Jandía Peninsula (➤ 84)

The dunes of Playa de Sotavento stretch for nearly 30km along the southern shore of the Jandía Peninsula

The sun-dried, windswept island has immense beaches and tranquil, empty regions of fabulous sand dunes.

Like a miniature Sahara, the island of Fuerteventura is sandy and waterless, windy and parched. For millennia sands have blown here across the 60 miles from Africa, covering the volcanic layer beneath, creating endless dune landscapes and great hills of pale sand.

Right behind Fuerteventura's main resort, Corralejo, on the island's northern tip, rises its largest and most impressive single area of dunes. This complex system of dazzling pale sands, stretching about 10km along the coast and reaching 2–3km inland from the shore, has been declared a protected zone known as the Parque Natural de las Dunas de Corralejo. Despite this conservation status, two popular package-holiday hotels stand within the park's limits, the Tres Islas and Oliva Beach. They pre-date the creation of the park.

Fuerteventura has another major dune area at the Isthmo de la Pared, the narrow isthmus of mountainous dunes separating Jandía Peninsula from the rest of the island. At some stage in prehistory, the dunes did not exist and Jandía was a separate volcanic island.

Fuerteventura's dunes are neither barren nor lifeless. As well as forming spectacular beaches, they also support unusual plant species that can thrive in these dry, salty sands. Some are found only here, including a yellow-flowering shrub, *Lotus lancerottense*, *Echium handiense* with its bluebell flowers, and a red-flowered succulent, *Euphorbia handiensis*.

4

Fundación César Manrique

César Manrique's own home, half submerged in a string of volcanic bubbles in the rock, displays to the full his tremendous artistic flair.

Manrique had a special interest in mobiles and one extraordinary example is the huge complex of colour and movement – like an enormous children's toy – standing at the entrance to his own home. It is best seen at night, when the mobile and the house are not so much illuminated as dotted with light.

Here architecture is fun, astonishing and brilliant. The visible exterior of the building, inspired by traditional local style, combines dazzling white with jet black. Around it, a garden of cacti, succulents and semicircles of stone is set between white and black walls. Immense cylindrical cacti look like green Doric columns. Above the doorway, note Manrique's 'logo' – an interlocked C and M said to resemble a devil.

Since Manrique's death, the interior has become an art gallery, made up mainly of his private collection. It includes works by most of the big names of 20th-century abstract and modern art, including Tapies, Miró and Picasso, as well as a number of Manrique's own powerful canvases.

Steps lead down into five volcanic bubbles (created during the eruptions of 1730–6), each made into a complete room with distinctive character, colour and furniture. One has a trickling fountain, another a palm tree growing up through the roof. The dining room has an open grill, a pool filled from a black waterspout, and a dining table beneath a ceiling of rock. Narrow galleries in the rock, painted white and black to match the rest of the house, link the bubble rooms.

Every detail of Manrique's home was lovingly designed – from the foundations to the chimney top

 29C2

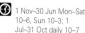 Taro de Tahiche, 5km north of Arrecife

 928 84 31 38

 1 Nov–30 Jun Mon–Sat 10–6, Sun 10–3; 1 Jul–31 Oct daily 10–7

Snack bar (£)

No 7 (Arrecife–Teguise), No 9 (Arrecife–Orzola), several times daily each way, stop at Tahiche

6 Avenida Gen Franco, Arrecife 928 81 18 60

Few

Moderate

Arrecife (▶ 31)

5
Islote de Hilario
(Timanfaya)

✝ 28B2

✉ Timanfaya National Park, 7km north of Yaiza

☎ 928 84 00 57

🕐 Daily 9–6 in summer, 9–5 in winter

🍴 El Diablo (££) restaurant and snack bar

🚌 None, but many coach excursions from the resorts

ℹ Avenida de las Playas, Puerto del Carmen
☎ 928 51 53 37

♿ Few

✋ Moderate (includes Volcano Route bus tour)

↔ Timanfaya National Park (► 54–61), Yaiza (► 73), Ermita de los Dolores (► 39)

❓ The last Volcano Route tour leaves at 4PM. For car drivers, there are extensive free parking facilities at the Islote de Hilario summit

The heart and soul of Lanzarote is an awesome red and black volcano called Islote de Hilario or Fire Mountain, whose presence dominates the island.

Lanzarote's Fire Mountain is still alive but taking a nap. Every visitor to the island is drawn to its summit. Visible from afar, the volcano dominates the view and the thoughts of visitors and locals alike. Its catastrophic force once destroyed in an instant the livelihood of most of the islanders, yet it is now Lanzarote's most stunning attraction. Of the several volcanic points in the island, including the other mountains of fire within the national park, this is the most terrible.

Black and red, fiery and ferocious, the swirling, sculpted terrain all around leaves no doubt that this is truly a volcano with a temper. Here and there tortured rocks are streaked with colour, where stones have melted and fused in the heat. The spectacular *malpaís* – badlands – all around the mountain show not a blade of grass, but do support lichen and small plants.

The usual way to climb the volcano is to drive along a roadway that climbs to the summit of Islote de Hilario, where the lingering volcanic heat remains hottest. At the very top, a big, crowded and convivial restaurant called El Diablo (The Devil) is an incongruous oasis of life and enjoyment amid the tortured, arid wilderness. Conceived and constructed by César Manrique, the restaurant is a glass-walled circle giving huge, thrilling views of the volcanic terrain and the sea beyond. Waiters serve delicious meat, bread and salty *papas arrugadas* and good Lanzarote wines.

Before you go into El Diablo, take a look at the wide opening resembling a well, just by the entrance. This 'well' descends into fiery earth, not water, and the restaurant's meat and fish are cooked in the oven-like 300°C heat that wafts up from the volcano. At other places close by, the surface of the ground is too hot to walk on, sometimes reaching 100°C. Ten centimetres below, the temperature is 140°C; at 6m down it is 400°C; while

Opposite: *the bleak landscape of Timanfaya National Park*

the temperature just 13m underground reaches 600°C.

Outside the restaurant's panoramic glass walls, uniformed staff of the Timanfaya National Park (► 55–61) make the volcano do impressive tricks: a bunch of brushwood thrown into a hollow quickly bursts into flames; a bucket of water emptied into a hole roars straight back as an immense spout of steam. In front of the restaurant buses set off on the round tour of the Route of the Volcanoes, included in the park ticket price.

When Timanfaya erupted in 1730, it threw a thick layer of burning rocks over the cornfields of western Lanzarote. During the six years that the eruption continued, the fertile western end of the island was devastated, and several villages in the Timanfaya area were burned off the surface of the earth. Today life has returned to normal at villages where the lava flow stopped, like Yaiza, Uga and Mancha Blanca, and the tiny pebbles of grey-black volcanic debris – *picón* – have been found greatly to aid agriculture, and are now being sold to farmers on other Canary Islands.

Water is turned instantly to steam by the subterranean heat

6
Jameos del Agua

✚ 29D4

✉ Near Arrieta, 26km north of Arrecife

☎ 928 84 80 20

🕐 Daily 9:30–6:45; also Tue, Fri, Sat 7PM–3AM (folklore show 11PM)

🍴 Restaurant (£££, evenings only), two bars (£, all day)

🚌 No 9 (Arrecife–Orzola)

♿ None

✋ Moderate

↔ Cuevos de los Verdes (► 17)

❓ Concerts and lectures held in the auditorium, and seminars in the Casa de los Volcanes. Details from tourist offices

Enjoy the experience of dining underground in this unique setting

César Manrique turned this bizarre volcanic feature into one of the island's most intriguing sights, an exotic subterranean water garden.

A *jameos* is an underground volcanic tunnel whose roof has partly collapsed. Until Manrique set to work, this one was just a hole in the ground.

Jameos del Agua is reached from the surface by spiral wooden stairs that twist down into the earth. At the bottom, astonishingly, a restaurant and dance floor look over an eerie underground lake; tiny, blind white crabs live in its perfectly transparent water. At the lake's far end, the arty tables of another bar perch on little terraces where you can sit with a meal or a drink.

This mysterious environment, within a roofless cavern below sea-level, is truly hard to comprehend at first. Whatever the weather outside, here the air is still and balmy, and full of the songs of tiny birds.

From the bar, meandering paths lead upwards among rocks and plant beds to a dazzling man-made blue and white pool. Behind it, a large cave accommodates a 500-seat auditorium used for shows, concerts and meetings! More spiral steps wind steeply up to the edges of the *jameos*, giving thrilling views down into this extraordinary meeting point of man and nature.

At the top, the Casa de los Volcanes (House of Volcanoes) is a science museum that is devoted mainly to volcanic activity.

After dark on Tuesday, Friday and Saturday, Jameos del Agua becomes a popular nightclub where crowds drink, dine and dance in the spectacular surroundings.

7

Jardín de Cactus
(Cactus Garden)

Manrique transformed a disused quarry into this extraordinary formal garden with over 1,400 varieties of cactus.

The fields of cactus around Guatiza and Mala, north of Arrecife, used to be cultivated as homes to a cochineal beetle, whose larva provides a bright red dye. Now the most striking landmark in the cactus district is César Manrique's towering 8m green metal cactus outside the entrance to his Cactus Garden.

Formerly a hand-dug quarry from which local farmers extracted volcanic rock, the garden is an oval-shaped enclosure descending in narrow concentric stone terraces. Each terrace is now covered with *picón*. Growing from the black ash like bizarre artworks are 1,420 species of cactus, a total of almost 10,000 plants, each standing separate from the rest and demanding attention.

Some are like porcupines, some like wedding cakes covered in hair, some like prickly rockets, some spreading themselves like octopuses, others uncoiling like snakes. Some resemble rolls of barbed wire. Others seem to have come straight out of a Wild West cartoon strip. Many have florid, gaudy blooms, others tiny, delicate flowers, sometimes strung around the plant like a necklace.

Visitors walk carefully around the terraces, gradually descending to a lower central area, where there is a miniature water garden and remnants of the quarry. A terrace rather wider than the rest accommodates a stylish bar, where circular wooden tables under pale sailcloth awnings offer a view of the entire garden.

Behind the bar, an old windmill rises above the garden and the surrounding landscape. Beautifully restored, it is still used for grinding grain.

A restored windmill rises behind the perfectly arranged cacti

29D3

Guatiza (17km northeast of Arrecife)

928 52 93 97

Daily 10–5:45

Bar/restaurant (£) 10–5PM

No 7 (Arrecife–Teguise)

6 Avenida Gen Franco, Arrecife ☎ 928 81 18 60

Few

Cheap

Teguise (► 25)

8
Mirador del Río

✛ 29D4

✉ 7km north of Haria

☎ 928 17 35 38

🕐 Daily 10–5:45

🍴 Snack bar (£)

🚌 None

🚢 To visit La Graciosa, catch a ferry from nearby Orzola

ℹ 6 Avenida Gen Franco, Arrecife ☎ 928 81 18 60

♿ None

✋ Cheap

↔ Haria (➤ 42)

Taking in the view across El Río

A touch of Manrique magic has made a clifftop view of little Isla Graciosa into one of the loveliest places on the island.

A *mirador* is a viewpoint, and El Rio, literally 'the river', is the name of the narrow strait between Lanzarote and its little sister island, Isla Graciosa. Outside the Mirador, one of Manrique's open metalwork signs stands in front of a daunting stone wall that actually conceals the view, with just a porthole hinting at what lies on the other side.

Before César Manrique set to work an old artillery post, Bateria del Río, perched here, 479m high on the Famara cliffs with a commanding view over La Graciosa and the islands of Montaña Clara and Alegranza beyond.

Manrique's first thought was to create a restaurant here. He had a large room chipped out of the cliff top, and roofed it with two domes covered with earth and grass. It is entered through a long, winding white tunnel and spiral staircase, which plays with brilliant effect on the themes of light, space and air.

The white room – or rooms, for the domes break up the space – is exquisite, its simplicity, clarity and spaciousness a delight to the eye. Neat wooden tables provide a place to sit and relax, and a most unusual-looking bar serves drinks and snacks. There is also a balcony, where you can stand in the open air by a sheer drop.

The main attraction, however, is the view itself, a spectacular vista of sea and sky, in which La Graciosa floats as if itself suspended like a sculpture.

9
Teguise

Lanzarote's former capital is today barely more than a village, but it still has the island's most elegant buildings and greatest charm.

Until 1852 this tiny town was Lanzarote's capital, in the centre of the island, out of reach of the coast's raiders and pirates. Founded in the 15th century by Maciot de Béthencourt, nephew of Lanzarote's Norman conqueror Jean de Béthencourt, it stands on the native islanders' ancient meeting point, known as Acatife. Locals still regard this as the island's real capital, while Arrecife remains *el puerto*, the port.

Though small, Teguise has an airy, confident Iberian colonial style with a handsome square, a grid of narrow cobbled streets and a church. For a hundred years it remained the Canaries' most important town, home of European nobility – the de Béthencourts, the Herreras and others – and gave birth to much Canarian folk culture, including its unique instrument, the *timple*.

In the white lanes and pleasant plazas of Teguise today, many buildings still possess a certain splendour. In the main square is the ancient, white-capped landmark church, Iglesia de Nuestra Señora de Guadalupe (also known as San Miguel), and the impressive Renaissance mansion Palacio

de Spinola (or Espiñola), former home of a wealthy 18th-century Genoese merchant, now a museum. The savings bank Caja de Canarios occupies a 15th-century tithe barn.

In the charming, smaller Plaza 18 Julio, the old hospital dates from 1473, and the snow-white, balconied Casa Cuartel, once an army barracks, from the 17th century. The two conventual churches, the Franciscans' 16th-century San Francisco and Dominicans' 17th-century San Domingo, are a short walk away.

Thousands of people arrive every Sunday for the morning market (➤ 106), one of the Canaries' largest.

Above: *the Church of Our Lady of Guadalupe*

🚩 29C3

✉ 9km north of Arrecife

🍴 La Galería (£), 8 Calle Nueva

🚌 No 7, seven times daily to and from Arrecife. Most tour operators run weekly coach trips to Teguise market on Sunday morning

ℹ 6 Avenida Gen Franco, Arrecife ☎ 928 81 18 60

↔ Castillo de Santa Barbara (➤ 37)

❓ Festivals at Teguise: 5 Jan (Cabalgata de los Reyes Magos); 16 Jul (Fiesta de Nuestra Señora del Carmen); 8 Sep (Fiesta de Nuestra Señora de Guadalupe)

10
Valle de la Geria

✚ 28B2

✉ East of Uga; along the
Uga–Masdache road
(LZ30)

ℹ Playa Grande, Puerto
del Carmen ☎ 928 51
33 51

↔ Yaiza (➤ 72–3),
Timanfaya National Park
(➤ 54–61)

❓ Wine-growers' *bodegas*
such as El Grifo and
Bodegas Mozaga offer
wine-tasting

*Vines are grown in
carefully sited hollows
dug into the volcanic
debris*

*The extraordinary vineyards in this blackened
landscape are dramatic evidence of the interplay
between nature's power and man's creativity.*

It might seem unlikely that a blasted rocky terrain covered
with grey volcanic debris would be among the most
intriguing and even beautiful of landscapes. At first sight,
the land appears hostile, barren and bleak. In places the
ground has been shattered by volcanic activity, sliced and
patterned by deep narrow fissures. Deep under the solid
surface, molten lava is still moving.

However, look carefully. Tiny white and coloured living
specks dot the dark volcanic stones – miniscule lichens
and tiny succulents. Unexpected dips and hollows harbour
little clusters of lush natural greenery. In spring the
roadsides are lined with wild flowers, some strikingly
coloured, like the purple poppies.

Most remarkable are the vineyards, each vine growing
deep in a separate hollow dug into the shingly earth. Each
hollow shelters behind its own semicircular rock wall. This
gives the vines just enough shade and shelter to survive,

and catch what little moisture
can be gathered through dew
and condensation. So
successful is the method, in
fact, that each produces some
200kg of grapes in a season.
Though cleverly functional, the
rows of little horseshoe walls
look more like art than
agriculture: César Manrique's
'landscape as art' has here
become 'farming as
geometry'. The vines produce
Malvasia grapes, and the wine
they make – fresh, dry whites
with a rich, pleasant flavour –
can be tasted and bought at
the various *bodegas* (wine
cellars) off the Uga–Masdache
road and in Uga.

When stopping to explore,
remember that the cutting
edges of the rough, sharp,
brittle black rocks and stones
make walking difficult and
unpleasant, and can destroy a
pair of shoes in minutes.

What to See

Above: boats in Arrecife Harbour
Right: harvesting onions near
Teguise

ISLAS CANARIAS

Madeira

P E

MA

DZ

MR

5

4

0   5   10 km

La Isleta
La Santa

3

Playa de la Madera

Tinajo

Centro de Visitantes
(Centro de
Interpretación)

Mancha   La
Blanca   Veg

Parque

El Volcán

Ermita de los
Dolores

Nacional de Islote de Hilario
Montañas
del Fuego
Timanfaya

Masdach

La Geria

2

El Golfo
El Golfo

Echadero de
los Camellos

Los
Hervideros

Uga

La
Geria

T

Mácher

Salinas
de Janubio   Las Hoyas

608m

Puerto
Carme

Las Breñas

Atalaya
de Femés

Femés

Puerto
Calero

Pl
Gra

Punta
Ginés

El Rubicón

Playa
Quemada

Bahía
de Avila

1

Playa
Blanca

Castillo de
las Coloradas

Punta
Pechiguera

Punta del Aguila

Playa de Puerto Muelas

Playa Mujeres
Playa de Papagayo

Punta de Papagayo

A

B

Roque del Oeste

Isla de Montaña Clara

Playa de las Conchas

266m
Las Agujas ▲ ● Pedro Barba

Isla Graciosa

188m
Montaña
del Mojón ▲

El Río

Punta Fariones

Caleta del Sebo

Orzola

Punta del Pobre **Mirador del Río** ■

Yé ●

Playa de Risco

Parque Tropical ■

Guinate

▲609m
Monte
Corona

Cueva de
los Verdes

**Jameos
del Agua** ■

Máguez ●

ta Guerra

Playa de
Fámara

**Mirador
de Haría** ■

Haría ●

Punta de
Mujeres

La Caleta ●

Urbanización
Fámara

670m
Las Peñas
del Chache

Arrieta ●

Tabayesco ●

Sóo ●

El Jable

Los Valles ●

**Jardín
de Cactus** ■

Mala ●

o Agrícola
io

Teguise ●

El Mojón ●

Guatiza ●

Teseguite ●

**Castillo de
Santa Bárbara**

Nazaret ●

raga

**Monumento al
Campesino,
Casa Museo del
Campesino**

Tahíche ●

**Parque
Acuático**

Punta de
Tierra Negra

San
Bartolomé

**Fundación
César Manrique** ■

Costa Teguise ●

ntaña
ca

Playa de las
Cucharas

Guime ●

Playa Bastián

Castillo de San José ■

ARRECIFE ■

✈ Playa Honda Castillo de San Gabriel

Playa de Matagorda
ya de los
illos

LANZAROTE

C

D

*Cactus flowers at César
Manrique's Jardín de
Cactus*

Lanzarote

Above all Lanzarote is about visual impact. Any idea that a little island devastated by volcanic explosions and blanketed with lava might not have much to see could hardly be more wrong. Lanzarote has so much to interest and amaze the visitor that every outing seems to be interrupted by constant pauses and photo stops. Some sights are the product of the power of nature alone, some are man-made, and some an intriguing combination of the two. It's fascinating to see how man's inventiveness has turned the volcanic activity to advantage, especially the covering of acres of good soil with *picón*, black volcanic grit that absorbs any dew or precipitation and helps crops flourish. Everywhere the hand of local genius César Manrique, self-styled 'ecological artist', can be seen, not just in major artworks and attractions, but in cottage architecture, colour schemes and design.

> *' We began to give back to the island its own original, volcanic character, emphasise its unique landscape and improve and impose a clear, sober, elegant and popular style of architecture. '*

CÉSAR MANRIQUE,
1981

Arrecife

Until the last century Arrecife was no more than a small working port. Inland Teguise was the island's capital and market centre, well away from the raiders who harried the coast. That's why Arrecife is still known to many locals simply as *el puerto*. To protect itself, Arrecife built the two fine fortresses that still watch over its harbours today. As the coastal danger declined and trade increased, Arrecife grew, finally becoming the capital of Lanzarote in 1852.

If, while touring Lanzarote, you ever wonder 'Where is everybody?', the answer is, 'in Arrecife'. Today half the islanders live in the capital, and many more come here to work each day. A striking, in some ways rather satisfying, contrast to the picturesque strangeness of the rest of the island, Arrecife is an ordinary, hardworking Spanish town making few concessions to tourists. Having expanded well before the days of César Manrique, this is the one place on the island that really does not conform to his aesthetic guidelines. Indeed, Lanzarote's most unsightly modern buildings are here.

There are pretty places too. Sturdy little Castillo de San Gabriel, standing on the reef that gave the town its name (*arrecife* means reefs), gives charm to the busy waterfront main road. The town's excellent El Reducto main beach and its old harbour, with the waterside gardens and promenade, are a delight. The other places of interest, too, are all close to the sea, and the main tourist office is also here on Avenida Gen Franco.

San Ginés Church is at the heart of Arrecife

What to See in Arrecife

CASTILLO DE SAN GABRIEL

Poised on a tiny islet called Islote de los Ingleses, just off the main town centre old harbour, Castillo de San Gabriel adds charm to Arrecife's waterfront. Built in 1590 by Italian architect Leonardo Torriani on part of the string of rocky islets off the town, the castle became a vital part of the defences protecting the harbour and town from marauding pirates. A low, sturdy, square and rather featureless structure, the castle is made more appealing by its honey-coloured stonework and the islet setting.

One of the most endearing features of the castle today – though it once had a serious military function – is that to reach it you must walk out along a walled mole. There is now a second causeway giving access for permitted vehicles, while the original is for pedestrians only. The causeway passes over a small drawbridge, known as the Puente de las Bolas – the Bridge of the Balls – because of the two cannon balls perched on top.

✚ 34C1
✉ Avenida Gen Franco
☎ 928 80 28 84
🕐 Tue–Fri 10–1, 4–7, Sat 10–1
🍴 Cafés (£) in Calle Leon y Castillo
🚌 From Avenida Gen Franco
♿ Few
💲 Free

Some weatherbeaten old cannon stand outside the castle. The view back towards the harbour and promenade puts Arrecife in a better light, with the white-capped San Ginés church belfry and the whitewashed houses of the little town standing out against the volcanic terrain beyond.

A small archaeological museum inside the castle has an assortment of historic items discovered locally, such as fossils and Guanche art.

CASTILLO DE SAN JOSÉ (➤ 16, TOP TEN)

EL CHARCO DE SAN GINÉS ⬤⬤

Sometimes mistakenly thought by visitors to be the name of Arrecife's old harbour, the Charco lies back from the sea within the town centre. This curious little lake or lagoon of sea water, surrounded by a walkway and modest fishermen's cottages, is said to lie at the very origin of Arrecife. The legendary San Ginés lived here as a hermit beside the water. A village of pious fishing folk grew around the hermitage, and as the village expanded into a town, the hermitage became the town's church. There are several such lagoons around the Lanzarote coastline, for example El Charco de Janubio (➤ 67) and the El Charco north of Costa Teguise (➤ 38); these have been put to use as salt pans, producing a coarse salt for preserving fish.

IGLESIA DE SAN GINÉS ⬤⬤

Arrecife's main church, this dignified little building of dark volcanic stone and bright white paintwork is dedicated to the town's patron saint. It was built in the 18th century when Arrecife was no more than a harbour village. Handsomely restored, the church is still at the old heart of the town, standing at one end of a pleasant square. Restoration has given the church a facelift, and inside it has an attractive Moorish ceiling. Formerly the hermitage of Ginés, it stands beside the El Charco lagoon, and to the locals their devotion to San Ginés is part of the town's marine tradition.

➕ 34C2
✉ Avenida Vargos
🍴 Cafés (£) on waterfront
🚌 From Avenida Gen Franco
♿ Few
🎫 Free

➕ 34C2
✉ Plaza de San Ginés
🕐 Open to public daily 9–1, 5–7 except during church services
🚌 From Avenida Gen Franco
♿ None
🎫 Free
❓ Annual Fiesta de San Ginés in August brings processions, parades and traditional dancing to the streets

Left: *El Charco de San Ginés is a seawater lagoon in the heart of the town*

Around Arrecife

The relaxed little capital of Lanzarote is where the real, modern life of the island is lived. Start at the tourist information office on the waterfront, an attractive pavilion made of volcanic stone and carved timbers.

Walk north, with the sea on your right, along the promenade as far as the causeway.

A narrow bridge leads onto the first of the causeways to the Castillo de San Gabriel (▶ 32).

Return to the promenade and take the road ahead, Calle Leon y Castillo. Turn right into the short street Calle Ginés de Castro y Alverez.

This comes to the church dedicated to San Ginés, Arrecife's patron saint (▶ 33).

Turn right and right again and follow the whitewashed lanes to the Charco de San Ginés (▶ 33). Follow the quiet promenade that runs all the way round the Charco, including a bridge across the entrance to the lagoon.

At the inland end of the lagoon short lanes lead back to Calle Leon y Castillo.

Turn left into Calle Leon y Castillo, towards the sea. Turn right at Calle Gen Goded and follow the direction of traffic along Calle Alferez Cabrera Tavio to Plaza de la Constitución. Cross the square to the far corner and turn left and right into Calle Luis Morote and follow this back street, with its glimpses of the sea.

On a busy corner dozens of café tables are set out beside Calle Dr Negrín. Ahead you can see the burnt-out Gran Hotel, Lanzarote's tallest (and ugliest) building.

Turn left along Avenida Mancomunidad. The road turns right and left to approach the promenade gardens and then to return to the tourist information pavilion.

Distance
5km

Time
2 hours

Start/end point
Tourist office
✚ 34B1

Lunch
Ciao (£)
✉ 1 Calle La Esperanza
☎ 928 81 35 11

Left: *the 16th-century Castillo de San Gabriel still guards the town's waterfront*

Below: *another golden sunrise over Arrecife Harbour*

What to See around Lanzarote

ÁGUILA ⭐

Standing on a promontory called Punta del Águila (Aguila Point), between the beautiful Playa Blanca and Playa Papagayo beaches on the island's southern shore, the restored circular watchtower called Castillo de las Coloradas (or Torre del Águila – Aguila Tower) stands guard beside the beach where de Béthencourt is said to have made his first landing on Lanzarote in 1402. In actual fact he had already dropped anchor in El Río and stepped on to the island of Graciosa. Another local story is that de Béthencourt himself erected the tower, though in fact it was built much later; it bears the date of 1769, and it is thought most of the present structure is even later, dating from 1778. There are good views from here across the straits to Fuerteventura.

ARRIETA ⭐

Arrieta is a relatively undeveloped, traditional small town of simple low white houses on the island's northeast coast; it is little known to visitors but nevertheless makes an interesting pause after a trip to the nearby Jameos del Agua (➤ 22) or Cueva de los Verdes (➤ 17). Its attractions include one of several fine beaches to be found along this part of the coast, and a picturesque harbour with a quay made of volcanic rock. On the waterfront stands the astonishing blue and red house (within a walled garden) of the **Centro de Arte y Cultura Africana** (Museum of African Art and Culture), celebrating the connection between the Canaries and the nearby continent.

➕ 28A1
✉ Playa Blanca
🎫 Free access
🍴 Many bars and restaurants (£–££) in Playa Blanca
🚻 Free
🔗 Playa Blanca (➤ 62–3), Papagayo (➤ 50–1)

➕ 29D3
✉ 22km north of Arrecife
🍴 Good fish restaurants (£) facing the jetty
🚌 Four times daily from Arrecife
♿ Few
🔗 Cueva de los Verdes (➤ 17), Jameos del Agua (➤ 22)

Centro de Arte y Cultura Africana
✉ On waterfront
☎ None
🎫 Daily 10:30–6:30. Closed Sun
♿ Few
🚻 Free

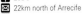

Did you know?

Why did de Béthencourt settle around Águila instead of El Río and Famara, where he had first arrived? For sailing ships, the trade winds were a danger on the north and west, while this southern coast is the island's most sheltered. Secondly, the flat southern plain gave much easier access to the interior.

CASTILLO DE SANTA BÁRBARA (OR GUANAPAY) AND MUSEO DEL EMIGRANTE CANARIO ★

A fine castle standing proudly on the summit of volcanic Mount Guanapay, overlooking the little town of Teguise, the Castillo de Santa Bárbara was for centuries a vital defence against Moorish raiders, who came inland as far as the island's old capital. The fortress was first erected in the 14th century by Lancelotto Malocello, the voyager who gave his name to the island, reconstructed 100 years later by Maciot de Béthencourt, and further strengthened in the 16th century.

Distinctive for its pale golden stone on an island where almost everything is either black or white, the castle dominates the area of villa developments around Oasis de Nazaret. The views alone amply reward a visit.

Inside the castle today an Emigrant Museum tells the stirring, sometimes tragic, story of how the poorest Canary Islanders have left in search of a better life. At times the people of Lanzarote emigrated en masse to South America. Among other things, we learn that natives of different Canary Islands settled in different countries. Lanzaroteños mainly went to Venezuela, while people from Fuerteventura emigrated to Cuba.

🕂 29C3

✉ 1.3km up a steep gravel track northwest of Teguise

☎ 928 84 50 72

🕐 Tue–Fri 10–4, Sat–Sun 10–2

🍴 Choice of restaurants (£) and bars (£) in nearby Teguise

🚌 No 7 takes around 20 mins from Arrecife to Teguise, with six buses each way daily

🚫 None

💷 Cheap

↔ Teguise (► 25)

On a clear day you can see for miles in all directions from the splendidly sited Santa Bárbara Castle

✚ 29D2

✉ On the coast 7km northwest of Arrecife

🍴 High-quality beachside bar-restaurants (££) on Playa de las Cucharas

🚌 No 1 from Arrecife every half an hour throughout the day Mon–Fri, every hour at weekends and festivals. Journey takes 20 minutes

♿ Good

↔ Arrecife (➤ 31–5), Fundación César Manrique (➤ 19)

Playa de las Cucharas, Costa Teguise's open, windswept main beach

COSTA TEGUISE ✪✪

Some maps of the island on sale in local shops still do not show Costa Teguise, or depict only a vague outline of a projected *urbanización* at the site. Within a few years this carefully planned, purpose-built resort town has sprung up alongside excellent beaches 5km up the coast from Arrecife. The quality of the accommodation and facilities is above the average for the Canaries, and represents good value for money, so Costa Teguise now attracts large numbers of holiday visitors, many of them self-catering.

Costa Teguise has also proved attractive to well-to-do Spanish and foreign celebrities, a number of whom have bought holiday homes here. But the resort feels unfocused and has an unfinished look in parts. Obviously there is no 'old quarter', and a string of *centros commerciales* and holiday apartment blocks backs onto the beach. Although everything is low-rise and has broadly been guided by the principles laid down by César Manrique, the new buildings are modern and charmless.

Yet what the resort lacks in history or character is made up for by a location ideal for sun, sea, sand, sport and sightseeing. In addition to the main, long, sandy Las Cucharas beach there are other enjoyable waterfront areas, including a second sandy beach with a rocky foreshore. Watersports facilities and rentals are available, and there's also an aquapark. An 18-hole golf course is just on the northern edge of town.

The Virgin of the Volcanoes in her church at Mancha Blanca

CUEVA DE LOS VERDES (▶ 17, TOP TEN)

ERMITA DE LOS DOLORES
(HERMITAGE OF THE SORROWS) ✪

Pilgrims flock to this beautiful church in the village of Mancha Blanca, especially on 15 September, the feast day of the Virgin of the Volcanoes. The village stands above the desolate *malpaís* at the point where it meets neatly farmed, highly productive fields layered with *picón*.

The Hermitage of the Sorrows – a gracious building with a cupola and a plain white interior – was built in honour of the Virgin of the Volcanoes, patron saint of Lanzarote, after she saved the village from destruction. It happened during the island's most recent volcanic eruption, in 1824, when lava and fire poured down from the Tinguatón volcano. The blazing liquid crept its way towards the village, igniting all in its path. Local people prayed fervently, begging Our Lady to spare them. The pious can prove that she listened to their pleas, for the lava flow did come to a halt – stopped, they say, by the Virgin's veil – at the very foot of Mancha Blanca village. The exact spot where the Virgin must have stood has been marked by a cross, placed at the edge of the *malpaís*.

In contrast to the miraculous intervention in the volcanic eruptions, Mancha Blanca also has an important National Park Interpretation Centre with a permanent exhibition on the vulcanology of the Canary Islands, and Lanzarote in particular (▶ 58).

🕂 28B3
✉ Mancha Blanca
🕐 Open all day every day; locked at night
🍴 Bar-restaurant (££) across the road
📖 Donations welcome
🔁 Islote de Hilario (▶ 20–1), Timanfaya National Park (▶ 55–61)
❓ Processions and celebrations on the Fiesta de la Virgen de los Volcanes, every year on 15 Sep

39

FAMARA ⭐⭐

Most tourist development has been on the sheltered southern and eastern coasts of the island, but the north coast has some glorious golden sandy beaches too. One of the very best is Playa de Famara – so good that visitors are prepared to put up with the slightly more temperamental weather and that little bit of extra wind that comes from the northwest. The ocean currents are also more dangerous here, so swimming and diving are discouraged, although windsurfers are drawn to this beach.

At one end of the beach, La Caleta de Famara – a small, working fishing village and low-key resort – makes for an enjoyable stroll, or even a good place to stay on this side of the island. It is particularly popular with anglers.

Rising behind the shore towards the other end of the beach, the spectacular Riscos de Famara (Famara Cliffs) rise an almost sheer 450m. These cliffs, with their exquisite sea views out towards Graciosa Island (► 43), continue – under different names – as far as the Mirador del Río (► 24) and beyond.

Above: playing on the vast sandy beach at Famara

FEMÉS ⭐

This likeable, secret little village on the back road to Playa Blanca rests on a ledge of rock among hills, with good views across the Rubicón plain to the south. Serious walkers reach an even better panorama by climbing the Atalaya de Femés, a 608m volcanic peak with breathtaking views to Timanfaya in one direction and Fuerteventura in the other. Femés was one of the first European settlements on the island, and the village church of San Marcial de Rubicón was the first cathedral to be built in the Canary Islands (► 68).

FUNDACIÓN CÉSAR MANRIQUE (► 19, TOP TEN)

EL GOLFO (THE GULF) ✪

On the southwestern shore of the island, El Golfo is the extraordinary result of a meeting between the blackened volcanic devastation of Timanfaya and the power of the Atlantic waves. Here the half-submerged cone of a volcano has been eroded and transformed into a bizarre natural attraction. Over time, the ocean has eaten into the volcanic crater, leaving a lagoon surrounded by an amphitheatre of lava cliff, the rock streaked and stained with a multitude of strange reds and russets.

Most remarkable is the colour of the lagoon. A number of factors, including volcanic minerals and algae, have given the water a deep, intense emerald hue, especially brilliant when it catches the sun, and a very striking contrast to the glorious blue sea that lies beside it.

Although linked to the ocean, the lagoon appears quite separate from it – the connection is through volcanic passages hidden underground.

To reach the lagoon, follow the access road on the left 2km before the village of El Golfo. On reaching the car park continue on foot, following signs for a short walk around the headland.

Between El Golfo village and the lagoon there are a number of sheltered bays with black beaches. The seashore village of El Golfo itself has rather an end-of-the-road feel, but has become a centre for enticing fish restaurants.

🞥 28A2
✉ 12km northwest of Yaiza
🍴 Restaurants Mar Azul and Casa Torano (£) in El Golfo village serve fresh fish and shellfish
🎟 Free
🡘 Los Hervideros (➤ 42), Salinas de Janubio (➤ 67), Timanfaya (➤ 55), Yaiza (➤ 73)

The green water of the lagoon contrasts sharply with the striated sandstone cliffs of the extinct volcano

29D3

15km north of Teguise

Snack bars (£) on the southern edge of town; Restaurante El Cortijo (££) serves classic Lanzarote dishes

No 7 from Arrecife; the journey takes about 1 hour

Arrieta (➤ 36), Mirador del Río (➤ 24)

Fiesta de San Juan celebrates midsummer on 24 Jun

Palm trees thrive in Haría village

HARÍA ★★

In contrast to Lanzarote's clichéd image as a volcanic island with a lunar landscape, here in the north of the island is a delightful little hill town in a lush green valley. Surprisingly, it is perfectly tranquil and unspoiled, with few visitors. The narrow streets and lanes are speckled with colour where purple bougainvillaea and red pelargoniums climb brilliant white walls. Stroll past some fine houses and pretty corners to reach a main square shaded by a canopy of leafy branches and loud with sparrows.

The setting of the village is especially striking, among a cool, green patchwork of fields and wildflower meadows shaded by palm trees. Poetically, this has been dubbed the Valley of 1,000 Palms – or even, sometimes, the Valley of 10,000 Palms! Some dispute the locals' claim that they have more palm trees here than anywhere else in the Canaries, but many plant species do grow in this valley that botanists have not found on any other Canary island. You'll see several types of cactus.

One of the best places to get an overview of this haven is from the Mirador de Haría, a high viewpoint beside the twisting main road as it hairpins round the heights of the Galería de Famara 5km south of Haría.

LOS HERVIDEROS ★

On the western shore, where the dark volcanic *malpaís* descends into the blue Atlantic waves, a *mirador* (viewpoint) looks across at a place where the ocean thunders in and out of sea caverns. The turbulent, bubbling effect has been called Los Hervideros, the boiling waters.

> ### *Did you know ?*
>
> *The names of Lanzarote's offshore islands suggest how they were seen by sailors after the two-day journey from Spain. Their first sight of land would have been the larger isles which were named Grace (Graciosa), Clear Mountain (Montaña Clara) and Joy (Alegranza). However, the dangerous smaller islet they called Hell Rock (Roque del Inferno).*

🔲 28A2

✉ 3km off Yaiza–Playa Blanca road

🍴 Nearby restaurants (£) in El Golfo, Janubio or Yaiza

↔ El Golfo (➤ 41), Salinas de Janubio (➤ 67), Yaiza (➤ 72), Timanfaya National Park (➤ 55–61)

ISLA GRACIOSA ★★

La Graciosa is the island that rests at the centre of the view from the Mirador del Río (➤ 24). For many who come to admire it, this is as near as they get to the island. However, La Graciosa is easily reached and a trip there makes an enjoyable day out.

Administratively, La Graciosa is part of Lanzarote. The channel (El Río) between the two islands is just 2km wide, though the ferry goes the long way round and takes 30–45 minutes. With a total area of only 41sq km, the island is small enough for keen walkers to walk round in a day; it welcomes few visitors and is haven of tranquillity.

Yet La Graciosa is not quite as deserted as might be thought. It has two sleepy fishing villages, Caleta del Sebo (literally 'Greasy Cove', named after the whale blubber found on the beach) and Pedro Barba, both on the channel between the two islands, as well as superb golden sandy beaches and a couple of simple bar-restaurants and basic *pensiones*. And the view from La Graciosa towards the Riscos de Famara and Mirador del Río is almost as good as the view from Lanzarote. Perhaps the island's most enjoyable feature is the lack of cars – no motor vehicles are allowed. There aren't even any roads.

Away from the shore, La Graciosa consists of dunes and treeless volcanic terrain. Despite this, it was at La Graciosa that Norman conqueror Jean de Béthencourt first stepped ashore after his journey from Europe.

🔲 29C4

✉ 2km off northern shore of Lanzarote

🍴 Two basic bar-restaurants (£) at Caleta del Sebo, near the ferry terminal

🚌 7:40AM bus from Arrecife to Orzola for the Graciosa ferry. Return to Arrecife on the 4:30PM bus from Orzola.

⛴ The daily morning ferry departs Orzola at 10AM and the last departure from La Caleta del Sebo is at 4PM. Don't miss it – unless you want to spend the night on the island

♿ None

↔ Orzola (➤ 50), Mirador del Río (➤ 24)

Exploring La Graciosa

Distance
18km

Time
4 hours

Start point
Caleta del Sebo
🚩 29D4
🚢 From Orzola at 10AM
🚌 To Orzola leaves Arrecife at 7:40AM

End point
La Caleta del Sebo
🚩 29D4
🚢 Back to Orzola at 4PM
🚌 Bus to Arrecife leaves Orzola when ferry passengers have disembarked, at 4:30–5PM

Lunch
Bars (£)
✉ Caleta del Sebo

Take the 10 o'clock ferry from Lanzarote to La Graciosa, which takes half an hour to reach La Graciosa's tiny port of Caleta del Sebo. The walk takes in Las Agujas (The Needles) and the Pedro Barba ridge, which form a mountain at the centre of the island.

Walk along the village quayside, then turn right (at the bar) on a footpath and then a dirt road towards the Pedro Barba ridge.

La Graciosa's two volcanoes stand either side of the track: Mojón to the left and Pedro Barba to the right. The third peak which comes into view between them is Montaña Clara, a separate island. Behind is a fine view of the village and Riscos de Famara.

At a fork keep right, and head towards the holiday homes at Pedro Barba.

You are walking around the foot of Pedro Barba volcano. The rocky island of Alegranza comes into view.

Where the track forks again continue on the left. The right-hand path heads down to Pedro Barba village, which makes an agreeable diversion.

The track skirts the northern slopes of Pedro Barba, with dunes away to the right, and a sea view of Alegranza. Ahead rises Montaña Bermeja, and the cone of Pedro Barba comes into view again.

La Graciosa seen from Mirador del Río

As the track heads away from Pedro Barba and towards the foot of Montaña Bermeja, take a turn on the left which leads you back in the direction of Lanzarote.

On the right is a spectacular beach of black rock and golden sand, called Playa de las Conchas. Ahead is the dramatic coast of Lanzarote.

A left turn takes the track south, again with Mojón on one side of the path (this time on the right) and Pedro Barba on the other. When the Riscos de Famara come into view, it's not much further to Caleta del Sebo.

ISLOTE DE HILARIO (➤ 20–1, TOP TEN)

JAMEOS DEL AGUA (➤ 22, TOP TEN)

JARDÍN DE CACTUS (➤ 23, TOP TEN)

MIRADOR DEL RÍO (➤ 24, TOP TEN)

MONUMENTO AL CAMPESINO/LA CASA MUSEO DEL CAMPESINO (MONUMENT/ MUSEUM HOUSE OF THE FARMER) ✪✪✪

The *campesino* is the countryman, the peasant farmer and man of the soil, whom César Manrique considered to be the very backbone of every nation, and the foundation on which its history and culture stands.

The white Campesino Monument is Manrique's tribute to the hard-working farming people of Lanzarote, who have long battled with the inhospitable terrain of their native island. Deeply moved by the labours that created the vineyards of La Geria (➤ 26), he named the 15m-high work *El Monumento Fecundidad al Campesino Lanzaroteño* (*The Fertility Monument to the Lanzarote Peasant*). Manrique dedicated the sculpture, which stands prominently at a road junction outside the wine village of Mozaga, 'to the forgotten endeavours of the unknown farmers of Lanzarote'.

The enigmatic cubist monument was constructed in 1968 from farm debris, water tanks and old fishing boats.

The Casa Museo del Campesino is a copy of a fine traditional farm building and farmyard presented as a pristine black, white and green artwork. You can see an old preserved kitchen, tools and equipment, as well as a reproduction of a cottage workshop. In keeping with Manrique's ideas, an attractive farm-style restaurant at the site serves Lanzarote dishes.

A traditional water-purifier displayed at the Campesino Museum

🏠	29C2
✉	Between San Bartolomé and Mozaga
☎	928 52 09 33
🕐	Daily 10–6
🍴	Restaurant (£)
	12:30–4
🚌	Nos 11, 12 and 13 to Tinajo, La Santa and Sóo
♿	Few
🆓	Free
↔	La Geria (➤ 26); Teguise (➤ 25)

Northern Lanzarote

Distance
66km

Time
5 hours

Start/end point
Arrecife
➕ 29C2

Lunch
Restaurants at Haría (££), and in the Mirador del Río (££)

This trip around the northeastern half of the island heads towards a Lanzarote that is awesome and yet pretty. Don't do this drive on Sunday, as the Teguise market brings thousands of people onto this route.

From Arrecife take the main road to Teguise. Note the Manrique mobile sculptures at the junction before Tahíche. César Manrique's extraordinary home is nearby (► 19).

Except for a strip of *malpaís* to the left of the road, most visible at Tahíche, the countryside is rolling hills of grass and, in spring, abundant wild flowers. As you approach Teguise, the hill of Guanapay, topped by Santa Bárbara Castle (► 37) comes into view. Teguise (► 25) deserves a leisurely visit on foot.

Follow the road to Haría, which soon begins to really climb and wind before descending to the town.

On the high plateaux and peaks there are windmills – not the picturesque and old-fashioned kind, but modern wind generators. The high, winding road is airy and enjoyable to drive along, with many outstanding views. In particular, beside a bar-restaurant at a mountain pass, is the beautiful viewpoint called Mirador de Haría (► 42). The descent into the green valley of Haría, dotted with palms, is delightful.

Now straighter, the road continues to Yé. Turn left here to Mirador del Río.

A lovely view of Haría from a mirador on the road

The Mirador del Río (➤ 24) deserves a stop. A narrow road to the left of the viewpoint is now closed to vehicles and makes a thrilling clifftop stroll.

Turn south again, at first on the same road; after 2km take a left fork and wind sharply downhill towards the coast.

Enjoying the sun and the view at Mirador del Río

Jameos del Agua (➤ 22) and Cueva de los Verdes (➤ 17) are nearby and well worth a visit.

Turn right onto the coast road, which skirts Arrieta (➤ 36), crosses the cactus fields and passes in front of the entrance of the Jardín de Cactus (➤ 23). At Tahíche, turn left to return to Arrecife.

Visit El Patio Agricultural Museum's prefectly restored windmill (opposite); all the components, including the wooden gears (right) have been lovingly crafted from traditional materials

MUSEO AGRÍCOLA EL PATIO (EL PATIO AGRICULTURAL MUSEUM)

●●●

In a suitably rural location at the centre of the island, this museum of rural life around 50 to 100 years ago gives an opportunity to see and learn about Lanzarote's intriguing, ingenious and unusual agricultural traditions. More than a museum, this is a peaceful, immaculately restored traditional farm, where visitors are guided round to take a close look inside one of the restored windmills and farm buildings, see a garden of cacti and other island plants, and contemplate the displays of farm tools, local architecture, ancient ceramics, and photographs of Lanzarote's traditional hard-working rustic lifestyle. To round off the tour, at the end of the visit you may taste wines actually produced on the estate.

ORZOLA

●

Close to the northern tip of Lanzarote, on the edge of the *malpaís* formed by La Corona volcano, this little working fishing harbour is the terminal for a twice-daily ferry to Isla Graciosa, the small offshore island that faces El Mirador del Río (➤ 24). Orzola makes a good base for keen anglers, and for those who would rather eat a fish than catch one, it's also an excellent lunch stop. There are good beaches nearby, too.

Did you know ?

The islanders developed an ingenious way of fishing without line, rod or net. The juice of the candelabra cactus was squeezed out of the plant and emptied into tidal pools when they were full of fish. Alive, but stunned by the juice, the fish became motionless, ready for collection.

🚩 28A1
✉️ 6km east of Playa Blanca on the coast road
🍴 Bar-restaurant (£) at Playa Papagayo
🚌 Nearest bus service is at Playa Blanca
♿ None
↔️ Playa Blanca (➤ 62–3), Águila (➤ 36)

PAPAGAYO ✪✪

Breezy Punta de Papagayo (Papagayo Point) and the more sheltered sandy bays either side of it lie at Lanzarote's southernmost tip. These are just about the finest beaches on the island: sweeps of fine golden sand edged by the clear waters of the channel separating Lanzarote from Fuerteventura. Oddly, these excellent beaches can prove hard to find, and some still have to be reached on unmade roads with few, if any, signposts to guide the driver. Despite this, they do attract plenty of visitors, and they can get almost crowded at times.

The main beach, Playa de Papagayo (*papagayo* means parrot), is barely more than 15 minutes' drive from the resort town of Playa Blanca. Thanks to a newly completed road straight from Playa Blanca (just continue a little way past Águila), this is the most popular beach.

The ruined hamlet of El Papagayo, which is also signposted, is now home to sun-loving hippies. A string of other lovely beaches stretching around the peninsula of Punta de Papagayo, backed by sandy cliffs, are best reached on foot: Playa de los Pozos, Playa de Mujeres, and beyond the point, the nudists' secluded favourite, Playa de Puerto Muelas or La Caleta del Congrio. Be warned, however: none of these beaches has any shade, so you will have to carry your own.

All along this sandy stretch of coast, there are superb views to Fuerteventura – and from high points on the cliffs you can even see Puerto del Carmen and Arrecife. It seems certain that as time passes this part of Lanzarote will become a major tourist centre. For the moment though, it remains fairly unspoiled and is strictly for beach connoisseurs and determined sun-seekers.

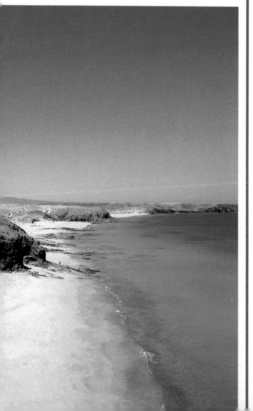

The secluded beaches of Papagayo are perfect for determined sun-lovers

Volcanoes

All the Canary Islands are volcanoes and were formed by volcanic eruptions, though at very different times. The oldest of the islands is Fuerteventura, which emerged from the sea with tremendous force some 20 million years ago. It was a full four million years later that the next major volcanic eruption brought forth another island from the sea, Lanzarote.

These two were the only two islands for another two or three million years. Gradually, the other islands were born, each with its own volcanic core.

Today the Canaries remain volcanic. Mount Teide on Tenerife was actually erupting as Christopher Columbus sailed by on his way to discover the Americas in 1492, and has had renewed outbursts of activity approximately every hundred years since – there could be another eruption at any time now. The most recent eruption was on La Palma in 1971, but it was relatively mild. While some island volcanoes are merely dozing, like Tenerife and Lanzarote, others have shown no sign of life for millenia, like Fuerteventura, whose volcanic terrain has broken down, and, to a large extent, been covered by wind-borne sand from the Sahara.

'Rope' lava being colonised by lichen and succulents

Lanzarote is the Canary Island that is the most physically and culturally dominated by its still-smouldering volcanic power. The eruption of Timanfaya and the other Mountains of Fire between 1730 and 1736 constituted one of the longest and most powerful periods of volcanic activity ever known. It totally devastated the southern third of the island, creating a blackened, lifeless *malpaís* of cinders, ash and lava. This was enlarged by another lengthy eruption from 1812 to 1824. Both eruptions considerably increased the overall surface area of the island.

The landscapes of Lanzarote and Fuerteventura clearly demonstrate the usual volcanic process of a single major cone creating a number of smaller cones all around as outlets for gases and liquids. Lanzarote also has many examples of underground tunnels formed by gas blowing

Escaping gases cause openings like this hornito *in Timanfaya National Park*

through molten rock, some of which have collapsed; for good examples of these, visit the Cueva de los Verdes (➤ 17) and Jameos del Agua (➤ 22).

The Lanzarote *malpaís*, both inside and outside the limits of the Timanfaya National Park, has good examples of all the various kinds of volcanic material thrown forth by volcanoes: pyroclasts (ash and dust particles); *picón* or lapilli (small solid particles); escoria, scoriae or pumice (lightweight fragments of rock shot through with air bubbles); bombs (large pieces of solid rock scattered about) and – most familiar of all – lava (liquid rock that flows along the ground and then slowly sets solid in ropey formations). Much has been discovered, too, about the way in which volcanic terrain is gradually colonised by flora and fauna from observing the encroachment of tiny lichens onto Lanzarote's volcanic surface.

Two outstanding places to learn more about volcanoes are open to the public on Lanzarote: the Mancha Blanca Visitor and Interpretation Centre (➤ 58), on the edge of the Timanfaya National Park, and the Casa de los Volcanes, or House of Volcanoes, at the Jameos del Agua grotto (➤ 22). Both have a wealth of displays, diagrams and models explaining how volcanoes work and how they created the Canary Islands.

How Volcanoes Work

Inside the earth, rock is a boiling liquid called magma. Where the surface crust is weak or broken, magma sometimes forces its way out through long hollows called pipes. Bursting out as solids, liquids and gases, it builds deposits into a volcanic cone. Eruptions can also break out of a volcano's sides or blow gases through underground tunnels.

MOUNTAINS OF FIRE

0 ___ 1 km

2

Parque Nacional
de
Timanfaya

Montañas del Fuego de Timanfaya

RUTA DE LOS VOLCANES

Mancha Blanca
Centro de Visitantes

Islote
de Hilario

510m
Timanfaya

Caldera
Rajada

▲ 377m
Montaña Rajada

437m

Valle de la
Tranquilidad

Casas de
Juan
Perdomo

▲ 256m
Pedro
Pericó

Montaña Encantada
246m

230m
▲
Montaña
Hernández

328m
▲
Montaña
Tremesana

1

El
Golfo

□ 175m

Islote de la
Vega

Yaiza

Echadero de
los Camellos,
Yaiza

Yaiza

A   **B**   **C**

Parque Nacional de Timanfaya (Timanfaya National Park)

Unlike most of the world's national parks, at first sight this one has no animal life, no birdlife, and not a blade of grass, flower or shrub growing anywhere. Instead the eye must become accustomed to a vast landscape of twisted and convoluted devastation. A stylised devil is the symbol of the park. With his horns, tail and trident, he conjures up a sense of mischief and fun, but while the Mountains of Fire may be fun to visit, they are a serious power. There are 36 volcanic cones within the park's 8sq km, and though they are peaceful enough at the moment, these volcanoes are still active. The black and grey desert of clinker and ash that surrounds the cones is the result of 26 eruptions between 1730 and 1736.

The start of those events was witnessed by a local man, the priest of Yaiza, Don Andrés Lorenzo Curbelo, who described them in his diary: 'On the first day of September 1730, between nine and ten at night, the earth suddenly opened close to Timanfaya, two leagues from Yaiza. During the first night an enormous mountain rose up from the bowels of the earth, with flames shooting from its summit, which continued burning for 19 days.'

A later entry in the diary recorded: 'On 18 October three new openings formed above Santa Catalina from which dense smoke emerged, which scattered over the entire island. The explosions which accompanied this phenomena, the darkness caused by the mass of grains and the smoke which covered the island, forced the inhabitants of Yaiza to flee their homes'.

Yaiza was lucky. Eleven other farming villages and hamlets were totally destroyed. Seventy years later, a series of earthquakes rocked the area again, culminating in the eruption of El Tinguatón volcano in 1824. The extraordinary terrain of Timanfaya was finally declared a National Park in 1974.

Left: *View from Yaiza, on the edge of the park*
Below: *Camels take tourists up the steep side of Timanfaya Mountain*

The Tremesana Route

Distance
3km

Time
2 hours

Start/end point
Visitor centre
🚌 54C2

Lunch
Take a packed lunch

Unregulated walking is not permitted in Timanfaya National Park for fear of walkers injuring themselves on the uneven terrain, or damage being caused to the fragile lichens that live on the surface of the volcanic rock. It has taken over 200 years for even this minimal flora to get established. There are two free guided walks supervised by the park authority. This, called the Tremesana Route, is the easier of the two. The visitor centre itself provides a fascinating introduction to this region (➤ 58).

The walk will start or end with a short minibus ride. From Yaiza, the group starts walking near the foot of Montaña Tremesana.

In this area, figs are cultivated, in stone half-circles to protect them from the wind (the trees, but not the ground they stand on, are private property).

Continue towards Caldera Rajada, ahead.

The volcano erupted from the side, splitting the mountain apart. The guide will point out amazing colours in the rocks, and explain how the eruption created hollow tubes just beneath the ground (which can be seen at close quarters at Jameos del Agua). Tell-tale signs, such as yellow sulphur stains, show the guide where these tunnels occur.

Below: *dawn over Timanfaya*
Right: *lichens eke out an existence clinging to the rocks*

The route continues between two other volcanoes, Hernández and Encantada. The guide will describe the process of plant colonisation.

The walk finally arrives at a track near the foot of a volcano called Pedro Pericó. You will be picked up by minibus and returned to the Visitor Centre by way of Yaiza (➤ 72).

What to See in Timanfaya National Park

ECHADERO DE LOS CAMELLOS (CAMEL PARK) ✪

Lanzarote's camels are actually dromedaries, but nobody's quibbling over what is really just an amusement for tourists. The camel park is a corral at the foot of Timanfaya, where visitors can wait in line for a 10-minute ride up the steep, unstable slag heap of the volcano. Each animal carries two passengers, who are strapped into wooden seats, one perched on either side of the camel. The camel train is then led up the slope by a guide.

ISLOTE DE HILARIO (➤ 20–1, TOP TEN)

State-of-the-art displays at the Mancha Blanca visitor centre

MANCHA BLANCA CENTRO DE INTERPRETACIÓN ✪✪ (VISITOR AND INTERPRETATION CENTRE)

Located on the park boundary, near the village of Mancha Blanca, the Visitor Centre must count as one of the park's most interesting sights – and one of the few man-made items in the landscape. The building at first appears small and low, its whiteness a sharp contrast with the dark lava. However, it turns out to be much larger, much of the centre lying underground. Inside is a cool, calm environment of white and black surfaces and polished wood, with exhibitions about the park, a library, bookshop, and administration areas, as well as viewpoints onto the volcanic terrain. Among the most interesting exhibits is the Eruption Hall, simulating the ground movements at the time of the 1730 volcanic eruption here. Note that no guides, no smoking and no noise are allowed at the centre.

MONTAÑA RAJADA ✪✪✪

Only to be seen on the Ruta de los Volcanes bus tour, which starts from the Islote de Hilario summit, this 350m peak gives one of the most awe-inspiring views of the park: a panoramic vista over volcanic cones and craters and the hollows caused by underground tunnels collapsing. Beyond, the blue sea makes a startling contrast.

MONTAÑA DE TIMANFAYA ✪✪✪

This, the largest of the park's volcanoes at 510m, is a vast dark cone that dominates the view throughout western Lanzarote. You can see it up close and admire the vivid red and yellow streaks (caused by mineral deposits) on the Volcanoes coach tour.

✚ 54C2
✉ 1km southwest of Islote de Hilario
🚌 On Ruta de los Volcanes coach tour (➤ 61)

PLAYA DE LA MADERA ✪

Where the park meets the sea there are inaccessible coves and black sand beaches. One of these can be reached by car on a track that is marked – very truthfully – Camino en Mal Estado (track in poor condition). The track can be reached from Tinajo, Mancha Blanca or a turn close to the Islote de Hilario entrance.

✚ 28A3
✉ 10km northwest of Mancha Blanca
🚌 None

The malpaís *meets the sea: the Timanfaya coast*

TIMANFAYA PLAIN ✪✪✪

The flat lowland that lies at the foot of the volcanoes is a sea of dark jagged rock, resembling the burnt out clinker after a coal fire; the terrain is so unusual that it deserves a good look.

✚ 28B2
✉ Between Yaiza and park entrance

VALLE DE LA TRANQUILIDAD (VALLEY OF TRANQUILLITY) ✪✪✪

In this part of the park some tiny bushes are trying to grow and a few tufts of grey-looking grasses manage to cling to the slopes, a hint of the future greenery that may one day take hold here.

✚ 54C2
✉ 1km south of Islote de Hilario
🚌 On Ruta de los Volcanes coach tour

Timanfaya Drive

Distance
30km, including 14km coach trip

Time
About 2 hours
Last coach trip at 5PM

Start point
Yaiza
➕ 28B2

End point
Mancha Blanca
➕ 28B3

Lunch
Restaurante El Diablo (££)
✉ Islote de Hilario
☎ 928 84 00 57

This drive crosses the *malpaís*, or badlands, and includes the official coach tour, which offers the only way to see the most awesome region at the heart of the park. The *Ruta de los Volcanes* coach tour departs at roughly hourly intervals throughout the day from outside the El Diablo restaurant on the summit of Islote de Hilario. The trip is included in the Islote entrance ticket.

From Yaiza drive due north on the Tinajo road. The dark, awesome malpaís *of Timanfaya Plain (➤ 59) starts almost at once. After 3km, the Camel Park (➤ 58) appears beside the road on the left. A further 4km brings you to the ticket booth for Islote de Hilario (➤ 20–1). There can be long queues here. Park at the summit of Islote de Hilario. Having watched the wardens demonstrate the intense heat of the earth just below the surface, take the coach trip*

around the centre of the 18th-century volcanic eruptions.

Although geared to tourists, and with certain special effects on board – designed to conjure up the atmosphere and power of the volcanic activity – you're unlikely to be disappointed by this extraordinary and memorable drive.

The coach takes a winding narrow road to Montaña Rajada (► 59), one of the most impressive viewpoints, looking out across volcanic cones, collapsed underground tunnels and a utter devastation reaching to the sea.

Manrique's volcano-top restaurant blends into the dramatic scenery

The landscape is not all dark – there are vivid colours in and around the volcanic cones. Below is the Valley of Tranquillity (► 59), which was buried in a downpour of volcanic particles.

Left: *some vegetation manages to survive in Valle de la Tranquilidad*

The bus skirts Timanfaya itself, and several smaller volcanoes, before returning to Islote de Hilario. After walking and exploring in the small area permitted around the Islote, continue to Mancha Blanca on the main road.

At Mancha Blanca visit the Interpretation Centre (► 58) and the Hermitage of Our Lady of Sorrows (► 39), a contrast between the scientific and spiritual aspects of the volcanoes' power.

61

🚻 29D4

✉ Guinate (4km from Haría)

☎ 928 83 55 00

🕐 Daily 10–5

🚌 Join an excursion organised from your resort, or go by car

⚫ None

👊 Moderate

↔ Haría (➤ 42), Mirador del Río (➤ 24)

🚻 28B2

✉ 35km from Arrecife

🍴 Bars and snack bars (£) and restaurants (£–££) on the promenade. Restaurante Brisa Marina (££) serves fresh fish, seafood and Canarian specialities

🚌 No 6 from Arrecife or Puerto del Carmen to Playa Blanca. There are about 6 departures daily, and the journey takes around an hour

🚢 To Corralejo, on Fuerteventura, several times daily. There are also ferries to Lobos Island, in between the two larger islands.

⚫ Few

↔ Timanfaya National Park (➤ 54–61), Los Hervideros (➤ 42), El Golfo (➤ 41), Águila (➤ 36)

PARQUE TROPICAL (TROPICAL PARK) ✪

The Tropical Park on the steep hillside behind the peaceful village of Guinate in the north of the island is an enjoyable and entertaining birdlife centre with over 300 species to see. The parrot shows are a particular treat.

PLAYA BLANCA ✪✪✪

This purpose-built – and fast-growing – resort on the island's southern shore basks in a sheltered position where both the wind and the waves are subdued.

The town's pleasant, golden sandy main beach catches the sun, is perfectly protected from the breeze, and is backed (in town) by an attractive promenade with plenty of greenery and café tables. There are two smaller beaches east of the centre, and another attractive beach area west of the port.

For the moment, Playa Blanca remains a quiet little place, with an away-from-it-all feeling that belies the fact that it is only 15km on a fast road across the Rubicón plain to Yaiza, and is therefore very conveniently placed for visiting Timanfaya National Park and all the sights of the southern half of the island. It's also handy for the west coast, where the volcanic *malpaís* reaches down to the Atlantic breakers.

From Playa Blanca's seashore you can look across the 11km channel between Lanzarote and Fuerteventura for a clear view of Fuerteventura and, in front of it, the small dark volcanic shape of Isla de Lobos. Ferries cross to Fuerteventura several times a day from Playa Blanca's main harbour for an easy and enjoyable day excursion. Fishing boats use the harbour too, and restaurants along the promenade feature plenty of freshly caught fish. There's also a bustling pleasure harbour.

The harbour area and the few streets to the east were the only part of Playa Blanca that existed before tourism took off here recently. West of the harbour, linked to it by another promenade, there is another new developement of shops, restaurants and accommodation, round a sheltered little bay of fine sand and gentle waters.

Playa Blanca is the furthest south of Lanzarote's resorts, a relatively long way from the sights in the north, but it has some clear advantages for those who want sun, sea and sand, good food and a peaceful atmosphere. With almost nothing here before the resort was built, it is dedicated to holiday enjoyment. Most entertainment is provided by the hotels, which in Playa Blanca are of a high standard. Set back from the promenade, attractive holiday apartment complexes and imaginatively designed, good-quality modern hotels are just a few paces from the sea.

Many visitors search out the more secluded sandy beaches to both the east and west, including impressive Playa Papagayo (➤ 50). To get your bearings, follow the coast round to the lonely clifftop Castillo de las Coloradas, which can be seen from anywhere in Playa Blanca. From here, in a beautiful sweep of coast, the great sandy bays of Papagayo can be glimpsed between the headlands reaching round to seen to Punta de Papagayo. The easiest way to visit the remoter beaches is to hire a small boat from the harbour at Maga Blanca.

The central beach in Playa Blanca is backed by an attractive modern promenade

PUERTO DEL CARMEN

URBANIZACIÓN
LOS MOJONES

CALLE DE LA REINA SOFÍA

CALLE DE JUAN CARLOS I

PUERTO
DEL
CARMEN

LOS
FARIONES

Centro
Atlántico

AVENIDA DE LAS PLAYAS

Playa Grande
(Playa Blanca)

A   B

Tuck into freshly caught fish at one of the local restaurants round the harbour

Puerto del Carmen

Lanzarote's main resort is surprisingly small and low-key. Yet it offers everything for a satisfying holiday: 5km of broad pale sand beaches, a wide choice of places to eat and stay, and an excellent base for reaching all the other sights of the island.

Puerto del Carmen is almost entirely a new town, a narrow strip clinging to the beach and dedicated to tourism. To the north it spreads out towards the airport and Arrecife, while at the other end of town the original fishing harbour lies south of the main beach. César Manrique's preoccupation with traditional, white, single-storey dwellings is less evident in tourist resorts, yet Puerto del Carmen has tried in its way to remain faithful to him. There are no high-rise structures, and almost all buildings, new or old, are white and unpretentious, even if they are not especially pretty or traditional in the way that Manrique might have preferred.

What to see in Puerto del Carmen

OLD HARBOUR

The small fishing harbour just south of Playa Grande was the heart of the original Puerto del Carmen village. It's still very much in use today, and gives character to this part of town; in the square next to the port, you can watch the locals playing *boules*. The local restaurants serve excellent fresh fish.

64A1

Western edge of town

Seafood restaurants (£) surround the harbour

Buses from Arrecife stop on Avenida de las Playas

Few

Below: *Relaxing on Playa Grande*

PLAYA GRANDE (PLAYA BLANCA) ✪✪✪

The town's main beach, a long, delightful wide band of yellow sand, runs alongside the busy Avenida de las Playas, the main artery of the town. Confusingly, it is often referred to as Playa Blanca, the same name as a quite separate resort at the southern tip of the island. On the beach side of the Avenida there's an attractive paved walkway with palm trees and gardens; across the street is a long strip of snack bars and restaurants, bright lights, tourist shops and places of entertainment. After dark, the Centro Atlantico along here is *the* place to find clubs and nightlife. The town's tourist office can be found in a hexagonal chalet beside the beach.

🔲 64A1
✉ Alongside Avenida de las Playas in western half of town
🍴 Restaurants (£) on Avenida de las Playas
🚌 Buses from Arrecife approx every half hour

PLAYA DE LOS POCILLOS ✪

A good beach some distance from the centre of town, Pocillos is where most of the lower-budget accommodation is to be found. Though it has its own disco, bars, restaurants and shops, on the whole it is quieter and less crowded. Pocillos is popular with local families as an alternative to the more hectic Playa Grande.

🔲 65C1
🍴 Restaurants (£) on Avenida de las Playas
🚌 Buses from Arrecife approx every half hour

PLAYA DE MATAGORDA ✪

Furthest from town and very near the airport runway, Playa Matagorda has fewer attractions and feels remote, yet is sandy and has a couple of good hotels. The beach is almost completely covered at high tide.

🔲 65D1
🚌 Infrequent buses into Puerto del Carmen

RUBICÓN   ✪✪

The southern coastal region of the island, known as the Rubicón, adds another element to Lanzarote's diversity. Lightly populated except for the new resort of Playa Blanca, the area resembles the sandy Fuerteventura rather than the rest of Lanzarote. However, this was the first part of the island to be settled by Europeans, Jean de Béthencourt coming ashore here in 1402 and constructing dwellings and a castle west of Playa Blanca. Femés (➤ 40) was one of the earliest settlements.

SALINAS DE JANUBIO   ✪

At several places around the island, alongside the coast, shallow seawater lagoons have been transformed into salt pans. One of the first, and still the most productive of these saltworks, was the lagoon at Janubio, on the southern edge of Timanfaya National Park.

The large salty lagoon, enclosed by hills, has been divided into fascinating neat rectangles subdivided very precisely into hundreds of smaller squares. As the water evaporates, the water changes colour and consistency, and ultimately dries away leaving large quantities of salt. Despite this very functional purpose, the salt pans look, like so much else on Lanzarote, as if they were intended primarily to be extraordinary works of art.

The salt is used in the island's traditional, and still important, fish processing and preserving industries.

Did you know ?

Lanzarote's salt pans traditionally played a surprising role in the islanders' health. Because farming was so difficult, fish became essential in the diet. But because fish were impossible to keep in the hot climate, dried and salted fish became important. Hence the salt pans – and the local speciality sancocho, *a stew of salt fish.*

LA SANTA ✪

La Santa is a popular little village in the middle of the rougher, less populous north coast, and is well placed for a lunch stop. It overlooks the curious low-lying peninsula known as La Isleta, which lies about 2km east of the village, cut off from the mainland only at very high tides. To reach the island, simply continue on the road past the entrance to Club La Santa.

La Isleta is home to one of the world's top private residential sports resorts, called Club La Santa: the facilities are available only as part of a full package holiday.

TEGUISE (➤ 25, TOP TEN)

✚ 28B3
🍽 Fresh-fish restaurants (£) in village
🚌 No 16 goes from Arrecife to La Santa in the morning and returns in the evening. It takes about an hour each way
  ♿ None
↔ Famara (➤ 40), Ermita de los Dolores (➤ 39)
❓ For more information on Club La Santa, call the Club's agents in the UK ☎ (0161) 790 9890

The geometric Janubio salt pans produce salt for dried fish

In the Know

To get a real flavour of the islands, here are some ideas:

(**L** = on Lanzarote; **F** = on Fuerteventura)

10

Ways to Be a Local

Eat *tapas*, which should be nibbled with an aperitif as a starter, or during the long hours between lunch and dinner. Eat lunch at 2 and dinner at 9 or 10.

Take a siesta. Life starts early and continues till late. Locals don't doze on a sun lounger all afternoon bu they do take a few quiet hours after lunch.

Dress with respect. Older islanders do not strip off in the sun. Most won't even wear shorts, but prefer neat dresses or trousers, and short sleeves. Many men wear a jacket even on hot days, and real leather shoes, too.

Drink espresso. Locals almost never drink milky coffee. At most, have just a dash of milk – that's a *café cortado* ('cut coffee'). It's OK, though, to have a *café con leche* (coffee with

Enjoy tasty snacks or a drink in a friendly local tapas bar

milk) for breakfast.

Eat doughnuts for breakfast and instead of using the usual southern Spanish name for them (*churros*), show you're an old hand by calling them 'donuts'.

Shout every word in a bar, bang the counter with coins and loudly call an already harrassed barman – in Spanish, of course. If you aren't a native, and don't have fluent Spanish, however, it might be better to be quiet and polite.

Knock the other islands. On Lanzarote, say that Fuerteventura is barren and windy. On Fuerteventura, sneer about Lanzarote's manicured beaches and elaborate attractions. On either island, tell everyone how overdeveloped and rainy most of the other Canaries are.

Forget about flamenco. Although tourist venues put on shows for guests, clichéd Spanish traditions like flamenco and bullfighting are not part of Canary Islands culture.

Buy a lottery ticket. These are sold by disabled locals, and buying one seems to be almost compulsory.

Never sunbathe. Locals stay out of the sun. On an especially fine spring day, a man might remove his jacket and sit out of doors – in the shade.

10

Good Places to Have Lunch

L Casa Miguel (£) Arrieta Harbour. ☎ 928 83 52 25. Quayside restaurant at the often-overlooked coastal town of Arrieta that serves good home cooking.

L Castillo de San José (££) ✉ Castillo de San José, Arrecife ☎ 928 81 23 21. The restaurant of Lanzarote's modern art gallery, inside an oceanside 15th-century fortress, is a typical example of César Manrique's imaginative style. Black nappery, white walls and good local dishes.

L El Diablo (££) ✉ Timanfaya National Park ☎ 928 84 00 57. Bright, busy focal point at the summit of Islote de Hilario (► 20–1). Panoramic views, and good traditional Canarian cuisine cooked over heat rising from the earth.

L La Era (££) ✉ Carretera General, Yaiza. The restaurant lies back off the road, and is signposted ☎ 928 83 00 16 Stylish yet rustic restaurant and bar in a 300-year-old Yaiza farm restored by César Manrique. House wine from their own vineyards.

L La Galería (£)
✉ 8 Calle Nueva, Teguise (by main square). ☎ 928 84 50 44. Relaxed, characterful place serving tapas, a range of fish dishes, stews and desserts.

L Los Helechos (£)
✉ At the viewpoint 5km south of Haría
☎ 928 83 50 89. At this restaurant you can feast on the superb view as much as the fresh fish and popular dishes.

F La Marquesina (££)
✉ Muelle Viejo, Corralejo, Fuerteventura ☎ 928 53 54 35. At the harbour. Relaxed and unpretentious place popular with locals. Fresh fish a speciality.

L Mesón La Jordana (££)
✉ Calle Los Geranios, Costa Teguise
☎ 928 59 03 28. La Jordana gives a local flavour to some international favourites.

F El Molino de Antigua (££) ✉ El Molino, Antigua, Fuerteventura ☎ 927 87 82 20. A restored 200-year-old windmill just outside Antigua offers tasty local dishes in a rustic setting.

L Punta Fariones (£)
✉ Calle La Quemadita,

by the harbour at Orzola. ☎ 928 84 25 58. In a neat blue and white building by Orzola's little harbour, this modest café-restaurant serves fresh fish and seafood at good prices.

Corralejo Beach, Fuerteventura

5
Top Activities

Tan: even in January there's an average of 8 hours sunshine per day. It's more in every other month. There's no better place to enjoy it than the islands' huge sandy beaches.

Windsurf: great beaches and stiff breezes create ideal conditions, especially on the coasts of Fuerteventura's Corralejo (► 80) and Jandía peninsula (► 84).

Dunewalk: walking on Fuerteventura's vast dunes is more like an expedition in a desert than a stroll on the beach (► 18).

Discover Manrique: his influence is all over Lanzarote, but the best place to experience his work is at his former home, the Fundación César Manrique (► 19).

Get into volcanoes: learn all about them at the Mancha Blanca Visitor Centre (► 58)

Stylish menu card from La Era restaurant

and see them in the Timanfaya National Park (► 55–61).

10
Top Beaches

L Costa Teguise (► 38), Costa Teguise, Lanzarote – narrow, but good

F Playa Barlovento (► 84–5), western Jandía, Fuerteventura – vast empty sands, not for swimming

L Playa de las Conchas, Isla Graciosa (► 43), off Lanzarote

F Playas de Corralejo (► 80), Corralejo, Fuerteventura – 10km long, backed by huge dunes

L Playa Famara (► 40), northwest Lanzarote, backed by high cliffs

L Playa Mujeres, nr Playa Blanca (► 62), Lanzarote

L Playa Papagayo (► 50–1), near Playa Blanca, Lanzarote

L Playa de los Pocillos (► 66), nr Puerto del Carmen, Lanzarote (another beach development lies next to it at Playa Matagorda)

F Playa de Sotavento, Jandía, Fuerteventura – gorgeous, 30km-long sweep of sand

L Puerto del Carmen (► 64–66), Lanzarote – the island's main resort with a great beach, Playa Grande

Southern Lanzarote

Distance
70km

Time
5 hours

Start/end point
Arrecife
➕ 29C2

Lunch
La Era (££),
✉ Carretera General, Yaiza
☎ 928 83 00 16

This is a fascinating and enjoyable day out, taking in the island's extraordinary variety and some of its most exceptional sights.

From the Arrecife city ring road (Circunvalación) take the turn to San Bartolomé. Stay on this rural road until you reach the junction with the road to Uga and Yaiza, on the left.

At this junction, close to the very centre of Lanzarote, is Manrique's strange cubist monument to the *campesino*, or peasant (➤ 48). Beside it is a small rural museum. Mozaga, straight ahead, has a good *bodega* (wine cellar), where you can buy local wines.

Take the Uga and Yaiza road. Beware – it becomes narrow, with deep ditches on each side. Passing is difficult in places.

This road enters La Geria, where vines grow in hollows dug into bleak grey volcanic desert. After 13km it reaches the attractive village of Uga (➤ 72).

At a junction, turn right for Yaiza, just 3km away.

Pretty white Yaiza (➤ 72–3) lies on the edge of the dark *malpaís*. Stop in the village for a walk and perhaps lunch.

Continue through Yaiza on the main Playa Blanca road.

After some 3km, on the right beside a junction, are the strange geometric salt pans of Janubio (➤ 67).

The road soon begins to cross the flat, rather bleak Rubicón plain (➤ 67). Follow it right into the resort of Playa Blanca (➤ 62–3).

Spend an agreeable half-hour on the promenade of this small, modern beach resort. For a bigger beach, and fewer people, explore Papagayo, down a coastal track east of town (➤ 50–1).

Take the less-frequented, minor road 6km

northeast towards Femés (➤ 40). Continue another 6km to the main road and turn right for Puerto del Carmen.

The road winds steeply down into Puerto del Carmen (➤ 64–5), a lively, pleasant family resort, with a big beach backed by restaurants.

Take the main road past the airport and back into Arrecife.

César Manrique loved the traditional, low, white-painted houses of Yaiza

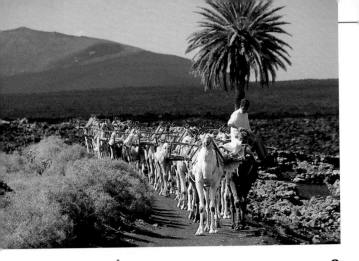

Above: *a camel train returns to Uga from Timanfaya*

UGA ✪

An incongruously green and fertile wine village on the fringes of the desolate volcanic terrain of the Timanfaya National Park, Uga stands at the western end of the bizzare La Geria vineyard area, where the wine bushes grow in volcanic rubble.

Despite the awesome location, Uga's simple single-storey white dwellings give it a neat, rather African charm. One of its main activities is breeding camels: not only do the animals that carry tourists up Islote de Hilario come from here, but also those that are used for safaris on the island.

If you want to see La Geria, drive out of Uga on the road to San Bartolomé via Mozaga, La Geria's main town and principal outlet for the region's wines. Be warned that in places the road becomes rough and very narrow.

VALLE DE LA GERIA (➤ 26, TOP TEN)

YAIZA ✪✪

This arty, yet unpretentious and picturesque old village of palm trees and dazzling whiteness, has often been described as one of the prettiest villages in the Canary Islands. It is dramatically located, facing golden hills one way, barren blackness the other. Standing on the very edge of the *malpaís*, it was all but destroyed in the Timanfaya volcanic eruptions of 1730–6. Just a handful of houses survived, but, as many surrounding fields and gardens were left intact, villagers slowly returned and rebuilt their homes.

The sunshine reflects brilliantly off their simple white-washed walls and houses. Some of the homes look prosperous and dignified, with little balconies and pleasing, flower-filled gardens. César Manrique wanted the whole island to look like this.

Accordingly, he set about his favourite task – providing

visitors with a good, stylish restaurant. He selected one of the pre-eruption survivals, a 300-year-old farm called **La Era**, and transformed it into a beautiful and fascinating complex of buildings and outbuildings. Enter it through a pretty little green-doored gateway into a quiet courtyard, off which a bar, a shop and a gardens form part of his restoration. The main area is a set of small rooms with white walls, and tables laid with attractive, loosely woven gingham cloth. The food is all Canarian specialities, and the crisp, tasty wine is made on the farm. But even if you aren't hungry, it's worth pausing to have a look inside this Manrique restoration.

While in the village, pop into the 18th-century church whose tower rises over the main square, Plaza de los Remedios, and visit the municipal art gallery at the Casa de Cultura or the **Galería Yaiza** art gallery. The latter exhibits local paintings and ceramics, and most of the work on show is for sale.

La Era Restaurant
✉ Carretera General
☎ 928 83 00 16
🕐 1–4, 7–11

Galería Yaiza
✉ On the Playa Blanca road
☎ 928 83 01 99
🕐 Mon–Sat 5–7. Closed Sun

Below: *typical low, elegant building in Yaiza*

Did you know ?

Yaiza, standing on the edge of the malpaís*, was almost entirely destroyed by Timanfaya's eruptions of 1730–6, and 11 smaller villages were wiped off the map. Yet despite the utter devastation wreaked by Lanzarote's volcanoes, it is thought that no one on the island has ever been injured during a volcanic eruption.*

Fuerteventura

A wild, unkempt golden desert island of sunshine and sand, Fuerteventura looks like a fragment of the Sahara. The island is almost uninhabited. Visitors exploring it find only light, peace, rocks of red and yellow and black, and wide open spaces. The sands have indeed blown here from the Sahara, and even the name Fuerteventura means 'strong winds'. Even so, eastern Fuerteventura is sheltered, though these coasts are famous for their windsurfing. In the interior and west, higher cones and ridges of darker rocks and vivid colours show the island's volcanic origin, though there hasn't been a murmur from these eroded volcanoes for thousands of years. Overall there's a sense that nothing at all has changed here in a long time.

> *'... an oasis in the desert that is civilisation.'*
>
> DON MIGUEL UNAMUNO
> (banished to Fuerteventura in 1924)

———————— ● ————————

Vast tracks of rippled dunes stretch down the coast from Corralejo

LANZAROTE & FUERTEVENTURA

0   20   40   60   80 km

Isla de Alegranza

Isla Graciosa

LANZAROTE

✈ **Arrecife**

Playa Blanca

Corralejo

Puerto del Rosario
✈

FUERTEVENTURA

**Las Palmas de
Gran Canaria**

GRAN CANARIA

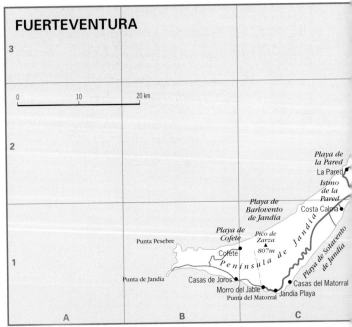

FUERTEVENTURA

3

0   10   20 km

2

Playa de
la Pared
La Pared

Istmo
de la
Pared

Playa de
Barlovento
de Jandía

Costa Calma

Playa de
Cofete

Pico de
Zarza
▲ 807m

Punta Pesebre

Cofete

P e n i n s u l a   d e   J a n d í a

Playa de Sotavento
de Jandía

1

Punta de Jandía

Casas de Joros

Morro del Jable

Casas del Matorral

Jandía Playa

Punta del Matorral

A   B   C

Punta
Martiño

Punta de la Tiñosa

Isla de Lobos

Corralejo

Punta de la Ballena

269m ▲
Bayuyo

*Playas de
Corralejo*

El Cotillo

Lajares

Parque
Natural
de las
El Jable
Dunas de
Corralejo

Playa del Aljibe de la Cueva

420m
▲ *Arena*

Villaverde

**Centro de
Arte Canario**

La Oliva

Casa de los Coroneles

Tindaya

Caldereta

Montaña Quemada 375m

**Monumento a
Don Miguel de Unamuno** ■

Vallebrón

Guisgey

Los Molinos

La Matilla

Tetir

Toma de Salinas

Tefía

Casillas
del Ángel

**PUERTO
DEL ROSARIO**

Llanos de la
Concepción

La Ampuyenta

Los Pozos

Playa Blanca
■ **Parador Nacional**

**Molino de
Antigua** ■

Triquivijate

El Matorral

Playa del Matorral

Betancuria

Antigua

Puerto de
la Peña

Vega de
Río Palmas

Los Pocetas

Caleta de Fustes

**Ermita de Nuestra
Señora de la Peña** ■

Ajuy

Valles de Ortega

Casas de
las Salinas

El Castillo de Fustes

708m
▲
*Gran
Montaña*

Casillas
de Morales

Playa del Castillo

Pájara

606m
▲
Carbón

Tiscamanita

Casas de Pozo Negro

382m
▲
Vigocho

Tuineje

*Malpais
Grande*

Playa Pozo Negro

Montaña
Hendida

Tesejerague

Punta de las Borriquillas

Huertas de
Chilegua

Gran Tarajal

Las Playitas

Peñón del Roque

Ginginámar

Gran Tarajal

Tarajalejo

La Lajita

Matas Blancas

D

E

F

Northern Fuerteventura

Distance
115km

Time
3–4hrs

Start/end point
Corralejo
✚ 77E5

Lunch
El Molino (££)
✉ Antigua
☎ 928 87 82 20

Carving around the doorway of Betancuría's interesting church

This drive passes through uninhabited areas of awesome space and emptiness, yet also fertile corners and picturesque villages. The main roads are good, but there's nowhere to buy petrol, so start out with a full tank.

> *From Corralejo take Route 600 due south into the interior, turning right after 7km at the first turning, which goes to Lajares.*

Lajares, a pretty village of white cottages, is noted for its embroidery and other traditional handicrafts.

> *Take the road to La Oliva, to a landscape of volcanic malpaís. On the left rises the soaring sandy mountain of Montaña Arena. The road reaches Route 600 again at La Oliva.*

The agreeable village of La Oliva (➤ 88) brings together the island's history and its variety of imposing terrain.

> *Follow the road south, passing Montaña Tindaya on the right. Carry on to the junction at the foot of the dark volcano Montaña Quemada, 'Burnt Mountain'. The Unamuno memorial (➤ 85) can be seen from the road. Turn right towards Betancuría. At a T-junction, keep right across a plain, passing several windmills. Continue into hills, climbing up before winding sharply down into Betancuría.*

Betancuría (➤ 79) has several interesting old buildings and deserves a leisurely stroll.

> *Return up the steep hill road to take the turn for Antigua (➤ 79), on the right. After exploring Antigua, visit the restored windmills on the main road on the way north to Puerto del Rosario (➤ 89). Turn onto the coast road north towards Corralejo.*

The road crosses stony terrain for some 10km before reaching Morro del Jable, a thrilling landscape of pale dunes designated as a Natural Park (➤ 18). Out to sea is the little island of Lobos (➤ 86). The road continues into Corralejo.

ANTIGUA ✪✪

Antigua dates back to 1485 and the early colonial period. Around the village much of Fuerteventura's historic character has been preserved. In the surrounding countryside windmills (*molinos*) still make use of the continual breezes to grind corn for the *gofio*, the roasted, milled cereal that is a staple Canarian food. The 200-year-old El Molino, on the main road heading north from the village, has been restored and converted into a craft centre. The grain store is now a restaurant. Further south at Tiscamanita is another mill and an interpretive centre, the **Centro de Interpretación de los Molinos**.

✚ 77E3
✉ 21km southwest of Puerto del Rosario
🍴 El Molino de Antigua (££)
☎ 928 87 84 82
🚌 No 1 from Puerto del Rosario to Morro del Jable six times daily
♿ None
↔ Betancuría (► 79)
❓ 8 September is the Fiesta of Our Lady of Antigua

Centro de Interpretación de los Molinos
☎ 928 85 14 00
🕐 Tue–Fri, Sun 9:30–5:30
💷 Cheap

Antigua's handsome 18th-century church also boasts a pretty garden

BETANCURÍA ✪✪✪

Named after the 15th century Norman conqueror of this island, Jean de Béthencourt – Juan de Betancuría in Spanish – this bright white village in the very centre of Fuerteventura remained its capital until 1834. Betancuría still keeps something of its historic, aristocratic character. De Béthencourt built his capital here in the belief that being so far from the sea, it would be safe from the Moorish pirates who terrorised the coasts. He was proved wrong; pirates repeatedly sacked the town, in 1593 destroying the original Norman-style cathedral and taking away 600 captives as slaves.

The church was rebuilt in 1620, in an interesting hybrid style, with a painted ceiling, a fine baroque altarpiece and ancient gravestones forming part of the floor. It became a cathedral again in 1924. Many village houses still have façades and doorways dating from the 1500s and 1600s. Across the church square, a museum devoted to religious art displays de Béthencourt's original standard, the Pendón de la Conquista. A **museum of archaeology**, across the (usually dry) river, houses Guanche relics, which are exceptionally plentiful here.

✚ 77D3
✉ 28km southwest of Puerto del Rosario
🍴 Simple bar-restaurant (£) beside Casa Museo; Restaurant Casa de Santa Maria (£££), by church
🚌 No 2 from Puerto del Rosario to Vega Rio Palma, twice daily
↔ Ermitage de Nuestra Señora de la Peña (► 81), Antigua (► 79)
❓ The major local saint's day is San Buenaventura, 14 July

Museo Arqueológico
✉ 12–14 Calle Roberto Roldán
☎ 928 87 82 41
🕐 Tue–Sat 10–5, Sun 10–2
💷 Cheap

CALETA DE FUSTES ✪

This up-and-coming new resort area receives large numbers of package tourists in mainly budget accommodation, having the advantage (or disadvantage) of being close to the airport. Several mid-quality small hotels and low-rise budget apartments have been built here recently and more are going up. There's a very good golden beach, a few lively bars and several inexpensive eating places. An 18th-century fortified round tower of dark stone, called simply El Castillo – the castle – stands next to a little pleasure harbour and has become part of a beach complex with restaurant, bars, watersports hire facilities, and a supermarket.

CORRALEJO ✪✪✪

Though still a working fishing harbour and a pleasant small town, this is Fuerteventura's biggest and most accessible beach resort. Lying on the breezy northern tip of the island, just across the narrow strait from tourist developments on the southern tip of Lanzarote, Corralejo has woken up to the fact that it too has that magic formula 'sun, sea and sand'. As a consequence, several hotels and apartment complexes are under construction. For sun, its record can hardly be matched anywhere else in the Canaries. When it comes to sand, although the sandy white beach in town is not very large, immense golden beaches and mountainous dunes stretch out just behind the town and go on for a long way (➤ 18). The heart of the town centres on a bustling square with shops, bars and budget restaurants, and there is a more bustling nightlife than in other resorts on Fuerteventura.

🚩 77E3
✉ 12km south of Puerto del Rosario
🍴 Selection of restaurants (£–££)
🚌 No 3 from Puerto del Rosario to Caleta de Fustes, via airport every hour
↔ Puerto del Rosario (➤ 89)

Above: *fishing in Corralejo Harbour*

🚩 77E5
✉ 30km north of Puerto del Rosario
🍴 Wide choice of restaurants (£–££)
🚌 No 6 via Puerto del Rosario, hourly; No 7 runs via La Oliva
🚢 To Isla de Lobos (30 minutes, ☎ 928 86 62 38); to Playa Blanca on Lanzarote (40 minutes one way, Fred Olsen Line ☎ 928 53 50 90).
ℹ Plaza Pública ☎ 928 86 62 35
↔ Isla de los Lobos (➤ 86), La Oliva (➤ 88)

80

EL COTILLO ★

This small holiday development around a fishing harbour on the windy west coast near La Oliva has black cliffs, sandy beaches, watersports and an 18th-century fortification called the Torre del Tostón or Castillo de Rico Roque. The air's fresh and clean and, though it's a popular excursion destination, there's an away-from-it-all feeling. Windsurfers like the wild waves at the southern beach; families and sunbathers prefer the gentler northern beach.

+ 77E5
⊠ 20km south of Corralejo
❙❙ Simple restaurants (£) near the harbour
🚌 No 8 to Corralejo every two hours; No 7 to Puerto del Rosario
↔ Antigua (► 79), Corralejo (► 80)

ERMITA DE NUESTRA SEÑORA DE LA PEÑA ★★

This small white hermitage brings to mind just the sort of isolation and remoteness one might expect of the Hermitage of Our Lady of Peña, tucked away in the hills outside Vega de Rio Palmas, just south of Betancuría. It's hard to reach, and getting there involves some stiff walking. The tiny building houses an alabaster statue of the revered patron saint of Fuerteventura. The third Saturday in September is her feast day, which brings crowds of islanders here for the all-important *romería*, the fascinating annual pilgrimage and procession.

+ 77D3
⊠ 5km south of Betancuría on the Pájara road
🕐 Tue–Sat 11–1 and 5–7, closed Sun and Mon
🚌 No 2 from Puerto del Rosario to Vega Rio Palma twice daily
↔ Betancuría (► 79), Pájara (► 88)

GRAN TARAJAL ★

Tarajal is the Canary tamarisk, numbers of which give a green aspect to this area and the valley of Gran Tarajal behind. Here on a south-facing shore, dark hills reach the sea at this small, charmless harbour village, which claims to be Fuerteventura's second-largest town. Untypically for the island, the fine sandy beaches have black sand. As well as tamarisk, the valley is noted for its date palms, which produce not only fruit, but also the raw materials for the island's ubiquitous straw hats and basketwork. Las Playas (or Las Playitas), a short drive up the coast, is another growing new development.

+ 77E2
⊠ 45km south of Puerto del Rosario
❙❙ Cafés and restaurants (£–££) on the beachfront
🚌 No 1 from Puerto del Rosario to Morro del Jable stops here, about six times daily
↔ Tarajalejo (► 89), Tuineje (► 89)
❓ Candlemas, on 2 Feb, is a big fiesta here, celebrated as the Fiesta of Our Lady of the Candelaria

Did you know ?

Now least inhabited of the Canaries (in terms of population per square metre), in Guanche times Fuerteventura was one of the most populous. It has more Guanche relics and sites than any of the other Canary islands. Though not always easily accessible, sites are scattered over a wide area, generally unmonitored, with free access. Tourist maps usually show them.

Food & Drink

Contrary to popular belief, food in the Canaries does not consist mainly of pizza, pasta and paella. For visitors who want to experience the real character and gastronomy of Lanzarote and Fuerteventura, there's plenty of indigenous food to be enjoyed. While the informal eateries in beach resorts do unsurprisingly tend to focus on international favourites, most inland restaurants offer traditional local cuisine. Look out for the word *tipico*, which roughly means 'traditional' or 'local'.

Malvasia
While other Canary Islands may produce wine, few can compete with Lanzarote's fine malvasia. Made of the grape that normally produces malmsey, Lanzarote's version – from the volcanic vineyards of La Geria – doesn't taste of fire and brimstone, as you might suspect, but has a delicious crisp fruity dryness, full of light and flavour.

Freshly caught fish on the Corralejo quayside

Mojo

One of the most genuinely Canarian words on the menu is *mojo*. Meat, fish and vegetables may all be served *con mojo* – with *mojo* – the piquant sauce that comes in different versions, more or less spicy according to what it accompanies. The two main types are *mojo verde*, green *mojo*, parsley and coriander giving a cool, sharp flavour, and *mojo rojo*, the spicier, red sauce made with chillis and peppers.

Gofio

The other most distinctively Canarian food is *gofio*. This staple of the Guanche diet is still very much in use. A rough roasted wholemeal flour (usually of maize, but possibly also of barley, wheat, or even chickpeas), it appears in soups, as a sort of polenta, as a paste mixed with vegetables, or as breads, cakes and puddings. *Flan gofio*, which resembles semolina pudding, has interesting African undertones. The people of Lanzarote and Fuerteventura are fond of hearty meat stews – sometimes with misleading names like Lanzarote's *potaje de berros* (watercress soup), in which the greenery may be barely discernible! Such rich, savoury soup-stews, usually combining several meats, including pork and rabbit, with chickpeas and vegetables and often thickened with *gofio*, are the main speciality; *rancho canario* and *puchero* (similar to French cassoulet) are typical, and especially popular for Sunday lunch. *El cocido* is Fuerteventura's version of these Canarian *garbanzos compuestos*

Dried fish, prepared in the Canary Islands as long as they've been inhabited, is still popular today

Cheese

Cheesemaking may be considered as not just production of a staple food, but as a local craft. Especially on Fuerteventura, the islanders are proud of their traditional Majorero cheese.

traditional stews (literally 'composed chickpeas'). Rabbit, *conejo*, is an especially popular and inexpensive ingredient on Lanzarote.

Vegetables & Fish

If you'd prefer something without meat, look out for *potaje*, vegetable stew. Fish soups include the well-known Canarian *sancocho*, a thick stew of salted fish and vegetables. Start your meal with *gambas al ajillo*, shrimps in garlic-rich olive oil, or *pulpo*, octopus. Main dishes tend to be plain and simple, such as grilled or fried fresh fish.

Thanks in part to the obvious difficulties of cultivation in this volcanic landscape, vegetables don't feature strongly in local specialities. But there are notable exceptions, in particular *cebollas* (onions); *batatas* (sweet potatoes) and tasty small *papas* (the local name for potatoes), which usually appear as *papas arrugadas con mojo*. Literally 'wrinkly potatoes', these are delectable new potatoes cooked in their skins with plenty of salt until the water has completely boiled away, sometimes served with a heavy sprinkling of crunchy rock salt – and *mojo*. Eat them by hand. *Batatas con mojo*, sweet potatoes in hot sauce, are an interesting alternative.

Desserts

Finish with a thick, chocolatey dessert, or corn cakes and syrup. Popular *frangollo* is made of *gofio* and dried fruit doused in syrup. Bananas are readily available, and for dessert are usually served fried or as *bienmesabe* – baked with chocolate and cream.

Malvasia wines on offer at El Patio Museum of Agriculture, Lanzarote

ISLA DE LOBOS

Lying some 3km offshore from Corralejo, the tiny Island of the Seals – as its name literally means – is a haunting miniature world, a curious landscape of tiny volcanic protrusions rising from stones and sand. Was it so named for real seals, as some claim? There are no seals here now. Perhaps instead the *lobos* were the little rock mounds, which do look from afar like animals lying on a beach. The once-volcanic Montaña Lobos, just 127m high, rises above the rest. Despite being a popular boat outing for tourists, the island has no roads, no vehicles and no inhabitants, and so remains an unspoiled haven of calm and simplicity (➤ 86).

77F5
3km off shore from Corralejo
Small café/kiosk (£) at quayside. Order lunch on arrival or take a picnic and plenty of water with you
Small ferry from Corralejo at 10AM, return boat at 4PM
Corralejo (➤ 80)

JANDÍA PENINSULA

In the south, Fuerteventura narrows at the sandy Pared Isthmus, before widening again to form the Jandía Peninsula, originally a separate island. An awesome land of vast skies and vast beaches, the peninsula is overlooked by Fuerteventura's loftiest peak, the 807m-high extinct Pico de Zarza volcano (also known – you'll understand why as soon as you see it – as Orejas de Asno, 'donkey ears'). All around the steep upland there are long wide swathes of pale sand and immense unspoiled beaches.

76C1
80km south of Puerto del Rosario
At Morro del Jable, numerous eateries (£–££) on the beachside promenade

On the peninsula's eastern shore, Playa de Sotavento de Jandía, or simply Sotavento, has 28km of sand. It's the site of the annual World Windsurfing Championships, though what makes this a windsurfer's heaven is being protected from the worst of the prevailing winds (Sotavento means 'leeward'). The unappealing Costa Calma development lies at one end of the beach.

South of Sotavento, the coast turns sharply west to the unsightly developments around Jandía Playa resort and to Morro del Jable, the peninsula's main town, which has a pleasant promenade, bars and eating places, and a fishing harbour. Beyond, the extreme tip of the island is edged with lovely, secretive sandy bays.

On the western side, the broad golden sandy sweep of Playa de Cafete and Playa de Barlovento ('windward') are beautiful but windy, with powerful undercurrents that are dangerous for swimmers. Inland, close to the shacks of Cofete, is the isolated mansion of Herr Gustav Winter, the enigmatic German owner of the whole Jandía Peninsula during and after World War II. Stories abound about Winter (who was given the land by General Franco) and his guests and his relations with the German, Spanish and Latin American regimes.

🚌 No 1 from Puerto del Rosario to Morro del Jable via all the resorts and beach stops of the eastern Jandía (six times daily); Nos 4 and 9, once daily each way, from Morro del Jable to inland Pájara (No 4 goes via Gran Tarajal, No 9 via La Pared), stopping at all the resorts; No 5 runs up and down the coast between Costa Calma and Morro del Jable about every hour from 9:30–9:30

🛳 A regular jetfoil service connects Morro del Jable with the islands of Gran Canaria and Tenerife

↔ Tarajalejo (► 89)

❓ Local fiestas on the Jandía Peninsula include 16 Jul at Morro del Jable, and the last Sat in Jul at La Pared (► 90)

The glorious sands at Sotavento Beach at Jardía, a surfer's paradise

Isla de Lobos

Distance
10km, plus ferry ride

Time
About 2 hours, plus about 1 hour on the ferry

Start/end point
Corralejo
✚ 77E5

Lunch
Picnic at the lighthouse

This curious offshore island has no restaurants and no shade, yet makes an enjoyable destination for a day out. Take a picnic, and be prepared for the breeze and hot, unsheltered sunshine.

Catch the island ferry from Corralejo at 10. It arrives at about 10:35. On arrival, head off to the right on the main wide track.

At once the track leads through rough terrain of lava and sand. The volcanic rock is streaked and coloured with little plants. On the right is the pretty, rocky Caleta de la Rasca bay, with views towards the dunes of Fuerteventura.

Follow the track through rocky and then sandier terrain. At a succession of little turnings, keep left on the track.

It takes less than an hour to reach the *faro* (lighthouse) at Punta Martiño, at the other end of the island. From here there's a great view back across Lobos and Fuerteventura and, the other way, to the pale beaches on Lanzarote's southern shore. This is the place to relax with a picnic.

Euphorbias are among the few, highly specialised, plants that can live in volcanic terrain

The track now heads towards the middle of the island, with the volcanic Montaña Lobos rising to the right of the path. At a right turn, walk away from the main track towards the volcano – there are other tracks off to right and left, but keep heading towards the crater.

After a few minutes' climb you reach the crater edge, from where there's a terrific view of both Fuerteventura and Lanzarote.

Back on the main track, follow it as it curves round to reach the beach near the ferry harbour. Walk on past the beach to get back to the ferry. The boat back to Corralejo leaves at 4, and arrives at about 4:35.

MONUMENTO A DON MIGUEL DE UNAMUNO ✪

At the foot of the volcanic Montaña Quemada, in the hills south of La Oliva, a monument records the exile to Fuerteventura of Miguel de Unamuno (1864–1936), the poet and thinker. While rector of Salamanca University, Spain's most distinguished place of learning, he was banished here in 1924 for his political views. He fell in love with the island's harsh, austere landscapes and lifestyle. Eventually de Unamuno returned to Europe and resumed his cosmopolitan life, yet in letters and poems often returned to the theme of love for the simplicities of Fuerteventura (➤ 89).

🟦 77E4
✉ Near the junction of Route 600 (the road to Corralejo via La Oliva) and Route 610 (the road from Puerto del Rosario to Betancuria)
🚌 No 2 (Puerto del Rosario to Vega Rio Palma)
♿ None
↔ La Oliva (➤ 88), Morro del Jable (➤ 84–85)

LA OLIVA ✪✪✪

Built in the early 17th century as a residence for Fuerteventura's military governors, this little town was the island's seat of government until 1880. Several fine old mansions, once homes of officials and wealthy land-owners, survive from those days, though some are now derelict. The grandest of them is the long white la Casa de los Coroneles (the Colonels' House) or La Casa de la Marquesa, dating from 1650 and once belonging to the Cabrera Béthencourt family – their family crest can be seen above the entrance. Near by, the surprising and enjoyable **Centro de Arte Canario** showcases modern art from the islands. A new attraction is the **Casa de la Cilla, Museo del Grano**, an old granary with a small exhibition.

On the road to Villaverde, windmills are a reminder that this area was a centre for production of *gofio*. North of the town rises sandy 420m-high Montaña Arena.

🟦 77E4
✉ 17km south of Corralejo
🍴 Cafés in village (£)
🚌 No 7 (Puerto del Rosario to Corralejo) stops here twice daily each way
↔ Monumenta a Don Miguel de Unamuno (➤ 85), Corralejo (➤ 80)
❓ Our Lady of Candelaria, is the big fiesta on 2 Feb

Centro de Arte Canario
☎ 928 86 82 33
🕐 Mon–Sat 10–6 (10–5 in winter). Closed Sun
🎟 Moderate

Casa de la Cilla, Museo del Grano
☎ 928 85 14 00
🕐 Tue–Fri, Sun 9:30–5:30
🎟 Cheap

The splendour of the Casa de los Coroneles has faded over the years, but many charming details – such as the intricate carving around the windows – survive

🕂 77D3
✉ 40km southwest of
Puerto del Rosario
🍴 Bars (£) in the village
🚌 Nos 4 and 9 from Jandía
twice daily.
♿ None
🔁 Hermitage of Our Lady of
Peña (► 81), Tuineje
(► 89)

PÁJARA ✪✪

The parish church of Our Lady of Regla at Pájara, in the island's western hills, is architecturally one of Fuerteventura's most important historic buildings. Built in sections – a roof beam in the presbytery is marked with the date 1687 – it has an altar that lovers of the baroque will appreciate. The fascinating decorations above the doors on the pink sandstone main porch are much older, and in a style believed to have been inspired by contact with the Aztecs. The village itself is shady and enticing, a rustic farming community in a pleasant fertile setting.

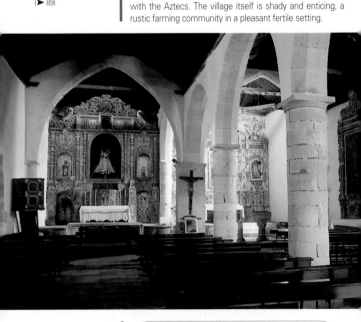

Iglesia de la Virgen, focal point of Pájara's 2 July Fiesta of Our Lady

Did you know ?

Like the French, the Spanish too have their Foreign Legion. Made up of tough soldiers accustomed to desert conditions, the Spanish Foreign Legion is based on Fuerteventura, at Puerto del Rosario. However, there is little for them to do and rather incongruously they can sometimes be seen on traffic duty.

PARQUE NATURAL DE LAS DUNAS DE CORRALEJO (DUNES OF FUERTEVENTURA, ► 18, TOP TEN)

PUERTO DEL ROSARIO ✪

Nothing stood on this spot until the early 19th century, and until as recently as 1956 this unprepossessing town and harbour still went under its accurate original name of Puerto Cabras ('Goat Port'). This seemed rather undignified for a capital city, however wretched, so the grander and prettier Puerto del Rosario was adopted. It became Fuerteventura's main administrative centre only in 1860, but today the harbour is the most important on the island, and around 80 per cent of Fuerteventura's population live here. Confirming its status, the airport was constructed here, too, just to the south of the town.

Beside the airport, the island's outwardly rather grim-looking *parador* (though inside it's as elegant and comfortable as is expected of this top-quality state-run chain) stands facing an equally grim looking beach, Playa Blanca.

TARAJALEJO ✪

Some tourist development has already started to attract people to this former small fishing village on the island's south-facing shore. Unusually for Fuerteventura, but like the nearby town of Gran Tarajal, the broad beach has dark-coloured sand.

TUINEJE ✪

At the heart of the island, and rather remote from the main tourist centres, this agricultural village keeps its rustic air and ancient Moorish appearance. In the main square, the altarpiece of the parish church has paintings of the Battle of Tamacita, when locals defeated English pirates. This event is commemorated annually on the 13 October. For the islanders, the village is worthy of note as a place that produces excellent goats' milk cheeses and the best tomatoes, which are grown in *fincas* all around the town.

Below left: *shell sculpture at Puerto del Rosario's harbour*

🔢 77E4
✉ 30km south of Corralejo
🍴 Café-bars (£) near harbour
🚌 Depot for the island's bus routes
🚢 Transmediterranean, ☎ 928 85 00 95, operates ferries to Arrecife (Lanzarote), Las Palmas (Gran Canaria) and Santa Cruz (Tenerife)
✈ Flights to and from Arrecife (Lanzarote) on Iberia (✉ Calle 23 de Mayo, Puerto del Rosario ☎ 928 85 08 02)
ℹ At the airport ☎ 928 85 12 50; in town, Patronato de Tursimo ✉ 33 Calle 1ero de Mayo ☎ 928 85 10 24
↔ Caleta de Fustes (► 80)
❓ Fiesta of Our Lady del Rosario, 7 Oct

🔢 77D2
✉ 62km south of Puerto del Rosario
🚌 No 1 (Puerto del Rosario to Morro del Jable)

🔢 77D2
✉ 32km south of Puerto del Rosario
🍴 Restaurants and cafeteria (£)
🚌 No 1 (Puerto del Rosario to Morro del Jable)
↔ Tarajalejo (► 89), Gran Tarajal (► 81)

Southern Fuerteventura

Distance
120km

Time
4hrs

Start/end point
Morro del Jable
➕ 76C1

Lunch
Simple fish restaurants (£–££)
in Gran Tarajal and Las
Playitas

This drive explores the wide-open spaces of the Jandía peninsula and the remote, simple towns of the rocky southern interior.

Leave Morro del Jable on the main coast road north (Route 640), passing through Jandía Playa's string of new development at the foot of Jandía's mountain peak, before swinging a few kilometres inland to pass the greatest of Jandía's beaches, Playa de Sotavento (➤ 84–5). Continue to the left turn for La Pared.

Before the Pared turn, roads on the right lead down to Sotavento beach. Just past the holiday development at Costa Calma, a turn leads into the Isthmo de la Pared, the Pared Isthmus. *Pared* means 'wall', and archaeologists believe these dunes marked the division between two Guanche domains – Jandia to the south, and Maxorata to the north. Before that, the Pared dunes did not exist, and the two domains were separate islands.

Las Playitas village, a quiet lunch stop north of Gran Tarajal

Follow the road to La Pared, and stay on it as it turns northward and enters volcanic mountain country. Don't stray off the main road as much of the land is an army firing range. Keep going to Pájara (➤ 88), then follow the road to Tuineje (➤ 89). Join Route 610 to get back to the coast at Gran Tarajal.

Gran Tarajal (➤ 81) is a good place to stop for lunch. Alternatively there is smaller, quieter Las Playitas about 6km further up the coast.

Return inland and turn left onto Route 640 for Tarajalejo (➤ 89). La Lajita is another ex-fishing village growing in popularity. Continue southward along the coast to cross the Pared Isthmus again and return along the coast road to Morro del Jable.

Where To...

Above: *holiday apartments at Morro del Jable, Fuerteventura*
Below: *one of Lanzatore's camels*

Lanzarote

Prices
Approximate price of a three-course meal for one without drinks.

£ = under 2,000 ptas
££ = 2,000–3,000 ptas
£££ = over 3,000 ptas

Meals with a View
Lanzarote has a number of restaurants with great views, including Castillo de San Jose (➤ 92), Los Cascajos and Mirador de la Valle (both ➤ 95). But for food and drink with an in-flight panorama don't miss Mirador del Río (➤ 95).

Arrecife
Campañitas (£)
A typical Spanish cafeteria in the commercial centre near the ring road, ideal for a drink, snack or a complete meal if you're shopping or exploring the island's capital.
🖂 Via Medular ☎ 928 81 19 19 🕘 8:30AM–9:30PM

Castillo de San José (££)
Inside the Castillo, attached to the modern art museum, and facing the sea through a panoramic window, this restaurant was designed by César Manrique as a work of art itself. There are black walls, black tables, even black napkins, and modern classical music playing. The food is sophisticated, well presented, with a moderately priced menu of the day. Can be visited without going to the museum.
🖂 Museo Internacional de Arte Contemporaneo, Castillo de San José , Carretera de Puerto Naos (3km north of Arrecife on main Costa Teguise road) ☎ 928 81 23 21 🕘 1PM–3:45PM and 8PM–11PM. Bar 11AM–1AM

Ciao (£)
Across the road from the sea at the start of the waterside gardens. The big, cool tiled interior of this typical Spanish bar-restaurant offers respite from the heat and noise, though there are also outdoor tables. A wide choice includes a modestly priced three-course meal including wine.
🖂 1 Calle La Esperanza ☎ 928 81 35 11 🕘 All day

El Pajar (££)
An attractive black and white exterior (and similar interior) of whitewash and volcanic stone compensates for a main-road setting opposite the landmark Gran Hotel tower. Paellas and pizzas are served as well as local meat, fish and seafood specialities and home-made desserts. Excellent value.
🖂 48 Avenida Mancomunidad ☎ 928 81 54 95 🕘 Lunch, dinner

Hotel Lancelot (££)
The restaurant of this pleasant hotel facing Arrecife's sandy beach is open to the public for very reasonable international cooking.
🖂 9 Avenida Mancomunidad ☎ 928 80 50 90 🕘 Lunch, dinner

Los Troncos (££)
This much praised shellfish and fish restaurant by the Naos port has interesting meat and fish dishes as well as well-known favourites.
🖂 9 Calle Agustin de la Hoz, Arrecife ☎ 928 81 36 37 🕘 Lunch, dinner

Arrieta
Casa Miguel (£)
This quayside restaurant in a simple little blue and white building at this often-overlooked harbour near Jameos del Agua serves good, unpretentious home cooking.
🖂 Calle La Noria, La Garita ☎ 928 83 52 25 🕘 Lunch, dinner. Closed Mon

El Charcón (££)
Popular bar-restaurant on the quayside. Food can be of variable quality (make sure yours is not just reheated) and service offhand.
🖂 Calle La Noria, La Garita 🕘 All day

Jameos del Agua (££)

When César Manrique turned this bizarre volcanic feature into a major tourist attraction, he added snack bars and a restaurant serving good Canarian cuisine. There could hardly be a stranger place to eat.

✉ **Jameos del Agua, beside sea near Arrieta (Haría district)** ☎ **928 83 50 10** 🕐 **Snack bars open all day; restaurant Tue, Fri, Sat 7PM–3AM (folklore show 11PM)**

El Lago (££)

About 10 minutes' walk from the town centre along the shore road, the restaurant has a fine sea view and offers a range of shellfish, fish and meat dishes.

✉ **On seafront north of harbour** ☎ **928 84 81 76** 🕐 **Weekdays 12–10, Sun 12–5. Closed Tue**

La Caleta de Famara
Bajamar Casa Garcia (£)

At the beginning of the village on the Famara side, this simple, satisfying little bar-restaurant is adorned with green trellis, hanging plants and check oilcloth tablecovers. The food is a tasty mix of local and European, with grilled *corvina* (translated as 'adlerfish', which doesn't help much) or veal escalope. Try following it with the *gofio* mousse.

✉ **Famara road, La Caleta de Famara** ☎ **928 52 85 76** 🕐 **All day**

Las Bajas (£)

Basic, but popular, meat and fish dishes, both inter-national and local, are served at this simple but charming eating place located on the edge of a genuine north coast fishing village.

✉ **Calle Callejon, La Caleta de Famara** ☎ **928 52 85 49** 🕐 **Lunch, dinner**

Casa Ramon (£)

Many visitors pause for a simple unpretentious Spanish lunch of fried fish, paella or pasta at this bar-restaurant beside the road into the village.

✉ **Calle Callejon, La Caleta de Famara** 🕐 **Lunch, dinner**

Costa Teguise
Bernardo's (££)

Attractively fitted out with various shades of green cane-chairs and glass-topped tables, this fish-oriented restaurant makes a pleasant open-air place for lunch next to the main beach. Enjoy *sama* (a local fish) in white wine sauce.

✉ **Centro Commercial Las Cucharas** 🕐 **All day**

Casa Blanca (££)

In a charming little detached building with a hexagonal roof, this unusual grill restaurant in the Jablillo area has a kitchen open to view and dark wooden tables on an enclosed terrace. Local fish dishes, salads and steak with peppercorns are among the choices.

✉ **4 Calle las Olas** ☎ **928 59 01 55** 🕐 **Dinner**

La Chimenea (££)

Good Italian food at the main beach. Relaxing decor of cool green and white motif outside, warmer orange and white inside.

✉ **Centro Commercial Las Cucharas** ☎ **928 59 08 37** 🕐 **Lunch, dinner. Closed Sun, Jul**

Restaurante Manrique

Several restaurants designed by César Manrique are based on a similar concept: a wide, low structure of sweeping curves, made of volcanic rock, with a panoramic window. But despite the similarities, each is styled to capture the sense of its location. And Manrique thought of every detail. Not only did he personally design the toilets at his sites, but even the rubbish bins were specially adapted for their particular place.

Costa Teguise Restaurants

Costa Teguise is divided into three distinct areas for dining purposes: Playa de las Cucharas, in the north of the resort; the busier area around Playa del Jablillo (including Plaza Pueblo Martinero); and the smaller Playa Bastián area at the southern end of town. There is a short drive between each of these these districts, and taxis ply between them constantly.

Columbus Tavern (££)

Catering for thoroughly British tastes, this laid-back bar-restaurant offers salads, spaghetti bolognese and home-made puddings – and a view of the main beach.

✉ **Centro Commercial Las Cucharas** ☎ 928 59 20 16 🕐 **All day**

Doña Lola (£)

Looking along the coast towards Arrecife, the terrace of this unassuming Playa Jablillo café-bar is a lovely place to enjoy a drink or a meal from an extensive menu of classic Spanish and international fish and meat dishes.

✉ **Centro Commercial Jablillo** ☎ 608 01 13 28 🕐 **All day**

La Graciosa (Melía Salinas Hotel, £££)

The smartest hotel on the island has an elegant restaurant open to the public. Entering on a wooden walkway through tropical gardens and over ponds where goldfish swim adds to the ambience. The food is sophisticated, mainly French, with giant prawns, or duck breast in plum sauce, but with local dishes too, like fish *à la sal con dos mojos*. Wonderful desserts. Live music.

✉ **Hotel Melía Salinas, Costa Teguise** ☎ 928 59 00 40 🕐 **Lunch, dinner. Closed Sun, Mon**

Mesón La Jordana (£££)

One Costa Teguise's best restaurants, with country-style decor and a menu that gives a local flavour to international cooking. Playa Bastían area.

✉ **Centro Commercial Los**

Geranios ☎ 928 59 03 28 🕐 **Lunch, dinner. Closed Sun, Sep**

Montmartre (£££)

A neon 'Moulin Rouge' on the roof is a reminder of the real Montmartre, as are the quarry-tiled floor, oil lamps and pink and white tablecloths. Fine French cooking, with duck liver pâté, and chicken stuffed with prawns with white wine sauce.

✉ **Avenida de las Palmeras, near corner of Calle Geranio** ☎ 928 59 12 05 🕐 **Dinner. Closed Thu**

El Patio (£)

A cut above the rest in authenticity, style, and the cooking of its Spanish and Canarian dishes. Tables are arranged under a green awning on their own terrace beside a crowded pedestrian square.

✉ **Plaza Pueblo Martinero** ☎ 928 59 09 45 🕐 **Lunch, dinner**

El Pescador (£)

Alongside a busy pedestrian plaza, this restaurant invites you to come inside and shut out the noise. Good service and an emphasis on seafood, which is reflected by the fishy decor.

✉ **Plaza Pueblo Martinero** ☎ 928 59 08 74 🕐 **Lunch, dinner**

La Provence (££)

A tasty muddle of Mexican, Italian, Spanish and, yes, some Provençal dishes at this popular grill restaurant. Gingham tablecovers do give a hint of France.

✉ **Avenida del Jablillo** 🕐 **Lunch, dinner**

La Terazza (££)

The menu at this bar-restaurant with outdoor tables is geared to holiday tastes. An extensive kids' menu at low prices.

🖂 **Centro Commercial Las Cucharas** ☎ **928 59 14 00** ⏱ **All day**

Vesubio (£)

At the seashore end of Avenida de Jablillo. Offers all the usual Spanish and foreign favourites on a terrace looking across the beach and down the coast towards Arrecife.

🖂 **Centro Commerical Jablillo** ☎ **928 80 46 75** ⏱ **All day**

El Golfo
El Golfo (££)

Simple fresh fish and shellfish dishes, as well as the ever-popular paella, between the sea and the *malpaís*.

🖂 **El Golfo** ☎ **928 83 00 89** ⏱ **Lunch, dinner**

Guatiza
Jardín de Cactus (£)

Beneath the windmill, big wooden tables under a sail-cloth awning. Enjoy a drink or a light meal and gaze at Manrique's amazing cactus collection.

🖂 **Jardín de Cactus, Guatiza (17km northeast of Arrecife)** ☎ **928 52 93 97** ⏱ **Daily 10–5**

Haría
Casa Cura (££)

Satisfying Canarian food prepared in an atmospheric old house with greenery inside and out. Several local stews like *sancocho*, *puchero* and *potaje* (➤ 82) served in little dining rooms.

🖂 **1 Calle Nueva (right turn off road to Yé and Mirador del Rio)** ☎ **928 83 55 55** ⏱ **Lunch, dinner**

Los Cascajos (£)

Just out of town to the north, with great valley views, this rustic restaurant has local speciality dishes and less expensive Spanish favourites. It's also a *bodega*, selling its own wines.

🖂 **9 Calle Maria Herera** ☎ **928 83 54 71** ⏱ **Lunch, dinner. Closed Sun**

El Cortijo (££)

In an attractive whitewashed converted farmhouse set back from the road, this popular restaurant serves classic Lanzarote dishes.

🖂 **On the Teguise road, at the edge of the village** ☎ **928 83 50 06** ⏱ **11–8**

Los Helechos (£)

At this big canteen-style restaurant you can feast on the superb view as much as the self-service snacks and light meals.

🖂 **At the viewpoint 5km south of Haria** ☎ **928 83 50 89** ⏱ **10–6**

Mirador de la Valle (£)

Enjoy a basic snack at this simple viewpoint location looking clear across the Haría valley. Approach slowly – the *mirador* is half-way round a hairpin bend.

🖂 **Los Valles, on road south of Haría** ☎ **928 52 80 36** ⏱ **Lunch, dinner. Closed Tue**

Mirador del Río (£)

Manrique's starting point when constructing this spectacular site was the bar-restaurant, and the *mirador* is essentially nothing more than a café with a view. Drinks, light snacks, and an exquisite setting.

🖂 **About 7km north of Haria** ☎ **928 17 35 38** ⏱ **Daily 10–6**

Volcanic Wines

Other Spanish wines come cheaper, but do try the local wine, red, rosé and white, the latter being especially good. It's made from *malvasia* (or malmsey) grapes, first brought to Lanzarote from Crete in the Middle Ages. Large-scale cultivation of the grape did not begin until after the Timanfaya eruptions of 1730–6: islanders discovered the grapevine was one of the only plants able to thrive in the volcanic debris. Each bush produces around 200 kilos of grapes per season.

Tapas One

Tapas bars are not a prominent feature of the islands, particularly in the purpose-built modern resorts, but you will find the occasional bona-fide *tapas* bar in the older parts of town and *tapas* (Spanish snacks) are also available in some traditional drinking bars and restaurants. This may be as informal as a few olives, cheese and a wedge of *tortilla* (potato omelette) or it can be a whole variety of dishes which combined make up a substantial meal. Some typical tapas are: *chorizo* (spicy salami-style sausage), *boquerones* (anchovies), octopus salad, prawn salad, Russian salad, *albondigas* (meatballs in a tomato sauce) and the ubiquitous *jamon serrano* (cured mountain ham). The latter either hangs from the ceiling or is placed on the counter in a special cradle-like holder ready for slicing. (▶ 98)

Isla Graciosa
El Marinero (£)

Visitors to the island can find food and refreshment at this bar-restaurant near the ferry terminal. Fresh fish and local wines are the specialities. It's even possible to pre-book a meal when you buy a ticket on the Romero ferry from Orzola.

✉ **Caleta del Sebo** ⏰ **Lunch, dinner**

Mozaga
Casa Museo del Campesino (££)

Beside the Campesino Monument and forming part of the museum, this attractive Manrique-built farm-style restaurant serves a wide range of traditional Lanzarote dishes, with much use of *gofio*.

✉ **San Bartolomé (on road between San Bartolomé and Mozaga)** ☎ **928 52 09 33** ⏰ **Lunch**

Nazaret
Lagomar (££)

An extraordinary setting carved into cliffs and connected to the ground by a tunnel and steps, with gardens, caves, a lake and walkways. Imaginative meat, fish and vegetarian dishes, mainly French and Italian in inspiration.

✉ **On main road between Tahiche and Teguise** ☎ **928 84 56 65** ⏰ **Lunch Tue–Sun. Dinner only on Thu, Fri and Sat. Closed Mon**

Orzola
Bahia de Orzola (£)

Blue and white cloths and paintwork mirror the marine location of this popular fish restaurant right on the dockside.

✉ **Avenida de Caleton** ☎ **928 84 25 75** ⏰ **Lunch, dinner**

Casa Arraez (£)

Rough red tables made from old rope spools stand on the quay at this place, which looks like a fisherman's shack. The set meal of Canarian stew and dessert, with bread and wine, is a bargain.

✉ **At the far end of Avenida de Caleton** ⏰ **Lunch, dinner**

Perla del Atlantico (£)

With a good position on the quayside of this working fishing harbour, and looking straight out to sea, this blue-and-white restaurant serves excellent fresh fish or grilled squid, with desserts that include *bienmesabe* (▶ 83).

✉ **Avenida de Caleton** ☎ **928 84 25 25** ⏰ **Lunch, dinner**

Punta Fariones (££)

In a neat blue and white building at the heart of the village beside the little harbour, this modest café-restaurant serves good fresh fish and seafood at reasonable prices.

✉ **Calle La Quemadita** ☎ **928 84 25 58** ⏰ **All day**

Parque Nacional De Timanfaya
El Diablo (££)

This broad, low, circular building beside Timanfaya's hottest hot spot is the busy focal point at the summit of the Islote de Hilario. The first of Manrique's landscape architectural works, it has panoramic views, and very enjoyable traditional Canarian cuisine cooked over heat rising directly from the earth.

Islote de Hilario, Parque Nacional de Timanfaya ☎ 928 84 00 57 🍴 Lunch

Playa Blanca
El Almacén de la Sal (£££)
Right on the waterfront in a converted salt store, this elegant, characterful place has a cool, attractive stone and timber interior. The wreck of a rowing boat hangs from the ceiling. Or sit on the shaded terrace outside, under big parasols. The menu offers the best of fresh fish and meat dishes, and many Lanzarote specialities. Live music at certain times.

 12 Paseo Maritimo ☎ 928 51 78 85 🍴 Lunch, dinner (snacks all day). Closed Tue

Brisa Marina (££)
Half-way along the waterside walkway of the old part of the village, this popular place concentrates on tasty fresh fish and seafood. Service can be offhand.

 10 Playa Blanca ☎ 928 51 71 53 🍴 Lunch

Puerto del Carmen
La Cañada (£)
Unassuming restaurant just off Avenida de las Mayas, serving up delicious local dishes.

 Calle de César Manrique 3 🍴 Lunch, dinner

Candil (££)
Steps decorated with black and white pebbles lead down to a beachside terrace under palm trees. This is a lovely spot, with good food and service, all at a reasonable price.

 28 Avenida de las Playas ☎ 928 51 03 05 🍴 Lunch, dinner

Cristobal Colón (£££)
Arguably Puerto del Carmen's best restaurant, this is surprisingly located in the Playa Matagorda commercial centre 10 minutes' drive from the centre of town. Elegant, tasteful, with impeccable service, and ornate tiles and pictures. Food is mainly French-style, ranging from fresh fish to the seven-course *menu gastronomique*. Wine buffs will be keen to treat themselves to somethng from the extensive wine list.

 47 Centro Commercial, Matagorda ☎ 928 51 25 54 🍴 Lunch, dinner

La Fontaine (££)
A fine selection of ambitious fish and meat dishes with emphasis on the local. Up the hill from the old port. It is advisble to make a reservation.

 9 Calle Teide ☎ 928 51 42 51 🍴 Dinner. Closed Tue

Lani's Bistro (££)
Airy, relaxed premises and a bustling corner location. No beach view, but a good place to watch the passers-by and enjoy an international range of dishes, desserts and pastries.

 24 Avenida de las Playas ☎ 928 51 23 02 🍴 10AM–midnight

Lani's Café (££)
The Lani group run seven differently styled restaurants along the Avenida, and they are among the town's best. This one has more international cooking than the others and specialises in cocktails.

 29 Avenida de las Playas ☎ 928 51 26 85 🍴 10AM–midnight

Eating out in Puerto del Carmen
There are said to be over 200 restaurants in town, mostly along the Avenida de las Playas. They range from Pizzerias to Balti to Tex-Mex. Few have any local specialities – Spanish dishes are likely to be gazpacho, paella and other mainland favourites. Restaurants often display photos of the dishes as well as a menu in four or five languages. Few restaurants accept reservations, so stroll along the avenue and chose one which takes your fancy.

Tapas Two

Although *tapas* should not be expensive it's as well to check the price in advance or as you are going along. It's quite easy to spend more on a succession of snacks than you would on a proper meal. Note too that some kinds of *jamon serrano* are very expensive. Locals sometimes display a curious litter-lout habit of throwing toothpicks, serviettes, sometimes even bits of prawn shell straight onto the floor by the bar. Unless you are a local don't copy them! (► 96)

Lani's Grill (££)

Good cooking and quick, polite service in several languages. With a rustic wood and ceramic interior, the Grill offers a wide range of meat and fish dishes.

📧 **Avenida de las Playas**
📞 **928 51 34 07**
🕐 **6PM–midnight**

Lani's Pizzerie (££)

A wide selection of authentic pastas and other dishes as well as the excellent pizzas.

📧 **38 Avenida de las Playas**
📞 **928 51 38 61**
🕐 **10AM–midnight**

Lani's Ristorante Italiano (££)

Tiled floors, lots of leafy ferns, purple tablecloths and a little bit of mock Roman decor make this a pleasant setting for good, authentic Italian cooking. Tasty hot rolls are served with garlic butter, and a complimentary liqueur is given after the meal.

📧 **29 Avenida de las Playas**
📞 **928 51 34 07** 🕐 **12–12**

El Mirador (£)

A perfect spot to enjoy a drink or a lunch with a wonderful sea view.

📧 **On walkway opposite Centro Commercial Arena Dorada, Avenida de las Playas**
🕐 **All day**

O Bota Fumeiro (££)

This excellent seafood restaurant on Playa de los Pocillos, near San Antonio hotel, is Spanish or French rather than Canarian in style. Try the *langoustines* or a *filet al roquefort*.

📧 **Calle Alemania, Centro Commercial Costa Luz, Avenida de las Playas** 🕐 **Lunch, dinner**

La Ola (£££)

Cool elegance and blue and white decor reflect a magical setting by the sea. Impeccable service and wonderful views. Start with *papas arrugadas* (► 83), choose from a traditional fish or meat main course, and finish with good ice-cream or cakes.

📧 **10 Avenida de las Playas**
📞 **928 51 21 32** 🕐 **12–12**

Pizzeria Italica (££)

A good choice for those staying at Playa de los Pocillos, which has fewer eating places, this thoroughly Italian restaurant has good charcoal-oven pizzas and tasty pasta.

📧 **66 Centro Commercial Jameos Playa** 📞 **928 51 16 66**
🕐 **All day**

El Sardinero (££)

One of the most highly praised fish restaurants on the island. A relaxed and informal place at the west end of the seafront (but with little or no sea view). Choose grilled sardines or *sancocho*, or just point out the fish you want – come early for a good choice.

📧 **9 Calle Nuestra Señora del Carmen** 📞 **928 51 19 33**
🕐 **Lunch, dinner**

La Terraza (££)

Animated place on busy corner specialising in delicious home-made ice creams and cakes; a wide range of cooked meals also available.

📧 **41 Avenida de las Playas**
📞 **928 51 32 19**
🕐 **9:30AM–midnight**

El Varadero (££)

Fishing boats pull up alongside this former

warehouse, which serves good *tapas*, fresh fish and traditional *papas arrugadas*.

✉ 34 Calle Varadero ☎ 928 51 31 62 🕐 Lunch, dinner

La Santa
Los Charcones (£)
On the main road skirting the village a couple of kilometres from the sports resort, this unpretentious restaurant has a strongly Spanish feel and specialises in locally caught fish and seafood.

✉ On Tinajo road ☎ 928 84 03 27 🕐 Lunch, dinner

La Santa (££)
Popular non-Spanish meat dishes like stroganoff, pepper steak, or *escalope Milanese* dominate a menu geared mainly to residents of nearby La Santa Sport.

✉ On Tinajo road ☎ 928 84 03 53 🕐 Lunch, dinner

Verde Mar (£)
Encounter the Lanzaroteños on their home ground and get a taste of the fried dishes they love at this basic bar in the village square.

✉ Plaza Iglesia ☎ 928 84 00 19 🕐 All day

Teguise
Acatife (££)
Ambitious and delicious cooking such as cucumber soup with smoked salmon, rabbit in red wine, charcoal-grilled meat, and Lanzarote wines, served in a restored historic building.

✉ 4 Calle San Miguel ☎ 928 84 50 37 🕐 Lunch, dinner. Closed Sun and Mon

La Galeria (££)
Relaxed, characterful place serving *tapas*, a range of fish dishes, stews and desserts,

with live music on occasions.

✉ 8 Calle Nueva ☎ 928 84 50 44 🕐 Lunch, dinner. Closed Sat

Uga
Casa Gregorio (££)
A traditional Lanzarote inn serving the Island's speciality dishes, including fried kid. On Sundays a traditional rich *puchero* stew is served.

✉ Uga 48 ☎ 928 83 01 08 🕐 Lunch. Closed Tue

Yaiza
El Campo (££)
Overshadowed by La Era's reputation, this is another good eating place in this lovely village, serving local and international dishes.

✉ By the football ground ☎ 928 83 03 44 🕐 9–11

La Era (££)
Excellent cooking of local specialities and a good value 3-course set meal are on offer here, in an agreeable old–fashioned atmosphere and delightful setting. The restaurant consists of a series of small rooms and tables laid with homespun gingham. The cool white Malvasia wines are made on the farm's own vineyard.

✉ Carretera General ☎ 928 83 00 16 🕐 Lunch, dinner

Yé
El Volcan (££)
This big, cheerful country-style restaurant is situated on the edge of Yé village in the hills near Mirador del Rio. Try the great mixed starter of *gofio*, figs, dried fish, sweet potatoes and goat's cheese, followed by grilled fish.

✉ Plaza de los Remedios ☎ 928 83 01 56 🕐 10–7. Closed Sun

Worth a Special Journey
La Era is not just a restaurant, and is worth visiting. Part of a fascinating complex of 300-year-old farm buildings and outbuildings, La Era is one of just three Yaiza builidngs pre-dating the 18th-century volcanic eruptions. It was beautifully restored under César Manrique's direction. A pretty little traditional green-framed gateway leads into a quiet courtyard, off which a bar, a shop and a garden form part of the same complex.

Fuerteventura

Wind from Africa

The Sahara sands that cover large areas of Fuerteventura have taken some time to arrive. Although windy on the island, most of the time the air is clear and comes from the north. However, when the sirocco blows, the dry wind from the east, it brings dust as well as heat. The 'dust' is in fact tiny particles of sand. The sirocco blows for short spells at a time, and mainly in winter.

Ajuy

Casa Pepín (££)

At this fishing harbour on the west coast, a short drive from Pájara, enjoy local dishes, including kid meat, fish and seafood.

✉ **Ajuy** ☎ **928 16 15 29**
🕐 **Lunch, dinner**

Antigua

El Molino de Antigua (££)

A grain store beside the restored 200-year-old windmill just outside Antigua has been turned into a rustic-style restaurant, offering tasty local dishes in a tranquil setting.

✉ **El Molino, Carretera de Antigua s/n, km 20** ☎ **928 87 84 82** 🕐 **Lunch, dinner. Closed Sun**

Betancuria

Casa de Santa Maria (££–£££)

Opposite the much visited church of Santa Maria, so something of a tourist trap, but still managing to serve enjoyable local food in an atmospheric old building.

✉ **Plaza de la Concepcion**
☎ **928 87 82 82**

Caleta de Fustes

Mona Lisa (££)

Good, varied menu of national and international dishes, huge pizzas and salads, and friendly, efficient service. A great place to take the children.

✉ **Urb. Puerto Caleta** ☎ **928 16 32 07** 🕐 **Lunch, dinner**

Corralejo

Café Latin (£)

A waterfront café with a choice of simple meals at tables actually on the water's edge.

✉ **21 Avenida Marítima**
🕐 **All day**

La Chama (£)

Excellent value fresh fish, grills, *tapas* and noisy locals kicking up a good atmosphere.

✉ **opposite Banco Santander**
☎ **no phone** 🕐 **Lunch, dinner**

El Corsario (££)

Spanish music rings out of this lively bar-restaurant. There's wood panelling inside, and a wood-covered street terrace with outdoor tables. Local dishes include a starter of Manchego cheese, *churros de pescado* (fried fish), and there are also foreign dishes like fillet steak with pepper sauce. Fresh-fish dishes priced by weight.

✉ **12 Calle La Iglesia** ☎ **928 86 71 65** 🕐 **Lunch, dinner**

Country Kitchen (££)

Traditional British food is on offer here, including fish and chips, steak and kidney pie, chilli con carne or chicken curry. Finish off with apple crumble. Portions are generous.

✉ **50 Calle Isaac Peral**
☎ **928 53 56 42** 🕐 **Lunch, dinner**

Fogelera (£)

Eat indoors or at tables on a beachside walkway with a view towards Lobos island, at this budget bar-restaurant with a Spanish feel.

✉ **End of Avenida Marítima**
🕐 **Lunch, dinner**

La Marquesina (££)

It is pleasant to sit at the outdoor tables of this relaxed waterside bar-restaurant close to the small jetty where boats pull up. Fresh fish a speciality.

✉ **Calle El Muelle Chico**
☎ **928 86 75 22** 🕐 **All day**

Il Mulino (££)

Authentic Italian cooking under a wooden arcade in a tiled alley by the harbour. Numerous meat and non-meat sauces to accompany fresh home-made pasta.

✉ **Calle García Escámez**
☎ **928 86 71 05** 🕐 **Lunch, dinner**

El Rincon de Perico (££)

Excellent *tapas* and half-portions as well as complete meals from a very authentic range of local dishes like *sancocho*, *gofio escaldo*, *potaje de berros*, *papas arrugadas*, and more.

✉ **40 Calle Gen Linares**
☎ **928 53 57 22** 🕐 **All day**

Rosie O'Grady's (£)

The best Irish bar in town, probably on the island. Live music every night and home-cooked food.

✉ **off Calle de Lepanto, four blocks back form the High Street** 🕐 **After 7PM**

El Sombrero (££)

Mock-rustic decor and a touch of style distinguish this good Mexican restaurant right on the harbour front. Sit indoors or outside by the water.

✉ **25 Avenida Maritima**
☎ **928 86 75 31** 🕐 **Lunch, dinner**

Sotavento (££)

Posters of the different kinds of fish and crustaceans help diners choose from an extensive seafood menu. Chops and steaks are also available. Smaller portions for children

✉ **19 Avenida Maritima**
☎ **928 53 64 17** 🕐 **Lunch, dinner**

Costa Calma
La Taberna (££)

A characterful, homely place in little rooms. Latin American and local cuisine, with *pescado a la sal*, fresh fish baked in salt, a popular speciality.

✉ **Carretera Jandía**
🕐 **Lunch, dinner**

El Cotillo
Playa (££)

Go down to the harbour of this small holiday development to enjoy the fresh fish and shellfish catch of the day.

✉ **El Cotillo harbour**
🕐 **Lunch, dinner**

Morro del Jable/ Playa Jandía
Saavedra (££)

Go downstairs in the commercial centre to find Spanish atmosphere and Spanish food.

✉ **4 Plaza Ciríllo Lopez, Jandía**
🕐 **Lunch, dinner**

Puerto del Rosario
La Marquesina (££)

A popular spot to enjoy the day's fresh fish and seafood dishes.

✉ **6 Calle Pizarro** ☎ **928 53 00 30** 🕐 **Lunch, dinner**

Parador Antiguo (£££)

One of the island's better restaurants in one of its least interesting locations (► 105)! Inside the slightly utilitarian state-run hotel, but open to the general public, the Antiguo offers a reliable menu of good food with Spanish and international flavours.

✉ **Parador de Fuerteventura, 45 Playa Blanca (south of town)**
☎ **928 85 11 50** 🕐 **Lunch, dinner**

Local Information

On Fuerteventura pick up a free copy of the small monthly listings magazine *Grapevine*, which has some useful resort maps, marked with places to eat, drink and be merry. There are also bus and ferry timetables and general information.

Lanzarote

Prices

For a double room, per night in the period Jan–Mar, booked independently, expect to pay:

£ = under 10,000 ptas
££ = 10,000 ptas–20,000 ptas
£££ = over 20,000 ptas

The Manrique Effect

Lanzarote lacks the high-rise hotels of other popular Canary Islands. César Manrique decided on a maximum five floors for hotels in a Zona Turistica (Tourist Zone). Even here, he laid down design guidelines which have been broadly followed. The result is a great success: a seafront not dominated by cheap concrete skyscrapers, but instead with unostentatious white buildings on a human scale, which retain a certain link with the island culture.

Most tour operators featuring Lanzarote offer a wide range of high-quality villas with pools as well as the small number of hotels listed here. Villas are ordinary modern houses – meeting the Manrique design criteria – in the new *urbanizacions*. The main areas for villas are Femés, Nazaret (near Teguise), Tías and Macher (both inland from Puerto del Carmen), and Playa Bastián (upmarket residential area of Costa Teguise).

Arrecife

Lancelot (££)

The modern, well-equipped Lancelot faces sandy Playa del Reducto beach, and is a 5-minute walk from the town centre. Cool and comfortable, this medium-sized, medium-priced hotel has a strongly Spanish feel.

✉ **9 Avenida Mancomunidad**
☎ **928 80 50 99**

Costa Teguise

Beatriz (££)

This hotel is some distance from the sea and the resort's centre. Black, white and red marble in the cool, spacious public areas reflects Lanzarote's colours. Amazing atria have waterfalls, a stream, lush greenery. Outside, a large swimming area has several pools.

✉ **3 Calle Atalaya** ☎ **928 59 15 13**

Meliá Salinas (£££)

Very stylish, with superb cactus gardens in front, this luxurious Las Cucharas beachfront hotel encircles wonderful watery tropical gardens inside. Rooms are of the highest standard, with beautiful bathrooms and sea views. Top-quality restaurant.

✉ **Avenida Islas Canarias**
☎ **928 59 00 40**

Teguise (££)

Hanging gardens and vast public areas with decorative pools welcome you into an extremely well-equipped comfortable modern hotel, well-placed in the Jablillo area of the resort.

✉ **Avenida del Jablillo**
☎ **928 59 06 54**

Los Zocos Resort (££)

Self-cater or eat in the pleasant buffet restaurant at this popular family holiday complex not far from the beach. Simple balcony (or terrace) rooms have a kitchenette, and TV is available. There's a safe, attractive pool area, nicely landscaped grounds and plenty of amusements for all age groups.

✉ **Avenida Islas Canarias**
☎ **928 59 21 22**

Playa Blanca

Lanzarote Princess (££)

This attractive, comfortably equipped hotel set back from the sea, is on the eastern edge of the resort, towards Papagayo.

✉ **Playa Blanca** ☎ **928 51 71 08**

Sun Park Apartments (££)

Just over 1km from the centre of Playa Blanca, 500m from the beach, this decently equipped two-storey complex caters for moderately priced package holidays. Choose to self-cater, or opt for B&B or half-board. There's a choice of pools, on-site supermarket, and simple rooms (no TV) with kitchenette.

✉ **Playa Dorada** ☎ 928 51 70 21

Timanfaya Palace (££)

The spectacular white exterior of domes, turrets, timbers and openings is modelled on traditional local architecture, while a curved frontage à la Manrique arches towards the sea. The lavish interiors are cool, comfortable and stylish. The hotel has a narrow but pleasant sandy beach in front, lined by a walkway.

✉ **Playa Blanca** ☎ 928 51 76 76

Puerto del Carmen
Los Fariones (££)

One of the island's older hotels, but very handsomely refurbished, the Fariones stands between Puerto del Carmen's old harbour and its long sandy main beach. A civilised tranquillity pervades the hotel, and the pool area and shaded waterside terraces are delightful.

✉ **Puerto del Carmen** ☎ 928 51 01 75

La Perla (£)

A simple, well-kept little hotel at the end of the beach and close to the old port; the bright rooms are equipped with private balconies.

✉ **7 Avenida de la Playas** ☎ 928 51 44 14

Riu Palace Lanzarote (££)

Hardly visible from the road, this elegant, comfortable low-rise hotel is set back from Playa de los Pocillos. Greenery, glass, marble and cacti give a cool, stylish air.

✉ **6 Calle Suiza** ☎ 928 51 24 14

San Antonio (££)

One of the original holiday hotels on the island, the Antonio stands in a quiet part of the resort, between Playa de los Pocillos and the resort's main beach. Pleasant palm and cactus gardens, heated outdoor pool; half-board only.

✉ **84 Avenida de las Playas** ☎ 928 51 42 00

La Santa
Club La Santa (££).

Near the village of La Santa on the breezy north shore of the island, this is one of the most highly rated sports resorts in the world. The tremendous range of facilities and full programme of sports amd sightseeing activities are reserved exclusively for guests staying at the resort. There are several swimming pools, including a 50m one, seven restaurants, a late-night disco, and extensive facilities for young children. Accommodation is in self-catering apartments and must be pre-booked.

✉ **Club La Santa, Tinajo** ☎ **In Lanzarote: 928 59 99 95. In UK: 0161 790 9890**

Yaiza
Finca de las Salinas (££)

This small inland hotel has plenty of charm. It's cool and peaceful inside, with flagstone floors and a lounge with cane seats arranged around palm trees growing through an open 'ceiling'. It has its own vegetable gardens and a small farm with animals. Near the Timanfaya road and almost opposite La Era restaurant.

✉ **17 Calle La Cuesta** ☎ **928 83 03 25**

Run for It

Although Club La Santa facilities can only be used by the sport resort's residents, outsiders may enter for the major international prize events held at or organised by Club La Santa, such as the Volcano Triathlon (1.5km swim plus 40km cycle plus 10km run) or the Ironman Triathlon (3.8km swim plus 180km cycle plus 42km run). Prizes can amount to £30,000 or more.

Fuerteventura

Book a Bargain
Most of the hotels listed are available as part of package holidays from tour operators, including return charter flights to the island. Some of the hotels can only be booked through travel agencies, and some only take half-board guests. If you're travelling independently, you'll usually pay more than package tourists – unless you're prepared to make a last-minute call direct to the hotels. Then, any vacant rooms will often be available at low prices.

On Fuerteventura the emphasis is on small-to-medium sized, modern, budget complexes of self-contained chalet-style family accommodation which combine self-catering apartments or chalets with a central reception area and some hotel amenities such as pools, play areas and restaurants. Principal self-catering areas on the island are Caleta de Fustes, Corralejo, Jandía, Playa Barca and the other developments alongside Playa Sotavento.

Caleta de Fustes
Caleta Amarilla Aparthotel (£)
About 1½km out of town, this plain and simple budget holiday apartment complex (actually two, separated by a road) offers chalet-style rooms with balcony or terrace, kitchenette, and all meals and drinks pre-paid on an 'all inclusive' basis.

✉ **Caleta de Fustes, Antigua**
☎ **928 16 31 25**

Castillo Beach Bungalows Sol (£)
The simple chalet-style self-catering bungalows at this popular budget complex are spread over a site with plenty of enjoyable facilities for family holidays, including several swimming pools with waterside bars, play areas, tennis courts and other games. The drawbacks are that there's overhead noise from the nearby airport, and it's 2km to the beach – but you can get there on a little shuttle train.

✉ **Caleta de Fustes, Antigua**
☎ **928 16 30 01**

Club El Castillo (£)
One of many low-rise, inexpensive aparthotel complexes, this member of the Barceló group offers accommodation in one- or two-storey simple beachside bungalows. Room facilities are limited but the reception area and public facilities include restaurants, bars, a disco, TV room, games room, swimming pools and a childrens' play park, as well as a handy shop for self-catering guests.

✉ **Caleta de Fustes, Antigua**
☎ **928 16 31 00**

Las Villas del Castillo (£)
This unusual, agreeable complex has 122 self-contained villas in a garden setting with palms and greenery, close to the beach. Each villa is effectively a hotel room with its own kitchenette and terrace, though there are no phones or TVs. The complex has its own attractive pool and sunbathing area.

✉ **Caleta de Fustes, Antigua**
☎ **928 16 30 44**

Corralejo
Los Delfines (£)
This simple, white two-storey complex of small self-catering apartments, each with its own little balcony or terrace, is attractively arranged around a pool area. The complex has a TV room, on-site supermarket, and some leisure facilities, such as squash courts. There's also a buffet restaurant, giving the option to eat out if preferred. Situated on the edge of Corralejo, some 200m from the beach.

✉ **Corralejo** ☎ **928 53 51 53**

Lobos Bahai Aparthotel (££)

An attractive pool and agreeable poolside bar are at the heart of this better-than-average complex of plain white two-storey buildings. All rooms have a kitchen area, balcony or terrace, and facilities include bars, restaurants, evening shows, TV room, games rooms, gym, and more, as well as a little supermarket for self-catering.

✉ Corralejo ☎ 928 86 71 43

Riu Oliva Beach (££)

A comfortable, well-placed family hotel with small rooms but good access to the vast, beautiful beach, a swimming and sunbathing area, and an all day children's club. Self-cater or choose half-board.

✉ Playas de Corralejo (south of town) ☎ 928 86 61 00

Riu Palace Tres Islas (£££)

Standing right on the immense beach that edges the dunes, this stylish, comfortable and well-equipped 365-roomed hotel is ideally placed for exploring the north of the island. Luxurious bedrooms have dark wood furnishings and private terraces looking over either sea or dunes. Palms and lawns surround a lovely swimming and sunbathing area.

✉ Playas de Corralejo (south of town) ☎ 928 53 57 00

Jandía
Los Gorriones Sol (££)

Beautiful, isolated position right on Sotavento beach with pools, sun terraces and gardens. Windsurfing school based at the hotel.

✉ north of Jandia resort
☎ 928 54 70 25

Iberostar Palace (£££)

The large, well-equipped new 4-star Iberostar complex has comfortable accommodation and an abundance of facilities for almost 900 guests.

✉ Urbanización Las Gaviotas
☎ 928 54 04 44

Mar Sol Apartments (££)

Dark hills and golden beach provide the setting for this pleasant apartment complex with its own pools, restaurant, sports facilities and play areas. There's nightly entertainment and a disco, and more entertainment and facilities in the centre of the resort, about 10 minutes' walk away.

✉ Morro Jable, Jandía
☎ 928 54 13 25

Puerto del Rosario
Parador de Fuerteventura (£££)

Stylish state-run *parador* (hotels) are found all over Spain, including most Canary Islands (but not Lanzarote). The one on Fuerteventura achieves the high standard of simple, polished elegance and comfort for which the chain is known. A rather unappealing barrack-like exterior is mitigated by attractive greenery. A less than ideal location between the airport and the capital town is likewise partly offset by the seashore setting. It has 50 rooms, a swimming pool and tennis courts, and the bar and restaurant are open to the public.

✉ Playa Blanca ☎ 928 85 11 50

Home from Home

Both Lanzarote and Fuerteventura have placed great emphasis on villa holidays, as a way of spreading tourists across a wider area, providing them with unobtrusive accommodation in the local style, and enabling them to contribute more to the economy.

Markets

African Traders
Colourfully dressed Africans in the market squares of Lanzarote and Fuerteventura bring an exotic note to the Spanish scene. These West African trading families, often Senegalese, make the boat trip specifically to sell in European markets, and stay for several months. Usually the whole family sits at different stalls selling very similar goods, or women may sit together grooming each other, breast-feeding, while older children tap idly at African drums.

Markets
Almost every town has its weekly or even daily market. These rarely have any of the fruit, vegetables or live chickens of traditional country markets elsewhere. Stallholders are usually Africans selling African handmade goods; northern Europeans selling their own craftwork; and Spanish market traders selling either linens, embroidery, lace and other cloth goods, or ceramics.

African Craftwork
Items for sale will include carved wooden masks, wooden toys, studded or tooled leatherwork and authentic African drums. In addition there are historic tribal artefacts, such as ancient ceremonial masks, which should perhaps not have found their way into the market. Nothing has a marked price. Don't buy ivory goods (illegal in the European Union) or cheap European and Far Eastern imitations.

Local Lace, Crochet and Embroidery
The most common items are tablecloths, placemats, napkins, bedlinen and handkerchiefs. These are by no means always cheap, but are good value for such high-quality handmade work, and have distinctively Spanish designs and character.

Ceramics
Tiles, glazed pottery and attractively handpainted crockery make excellent gifts or souvenirs but can be heavy and fragile for air-travellers. However, small items, well-packed, make a distinctive and worthwhile purchase.

Teguise
The main shopping event for many visitors is the Sunday market in Teguise, which operates from 9AM to 2PM, and is one of the Canaries' largest. A vast array of stalls, surrounded by shoppers, is crammed into almost every inch of the little town. Thousands of tourists are brought by special buses from resorts all around the island to see the market, and countless others come in by rented car or even on foot, until Teguise is bursting with the crowd. The carnival-like atmosphere is often enhanced by colourful folklore shows and traditional events.

Other Markets
Arrecife
Saturday morning at El Charco de San Ginés

Costa Teguise
Friday afternoon in Plaza Pueblo Marinero

Playa Blanca
Wednesday morning in Punta Limones commercial centre.

Marcha Blanca
During the Mancha Blanca fiesta (▶ 39) in September there is a big street market of traders from all of the Canary Islands.

Duty Free Shopping
The Canary Islands are a big duty-free region, selling perfumes, cameras, binoculars and other optical goods, CD players

Duty Free Shopping & Souvenirs

and electronic items, at low prices. In the big towns and main resorts, several shops specialise in these goods. Prices are similar to those in airport shops and other duty-free outlets. Watch out, however, for watches with fake designer names. Alcohol of all types is an especially cheap buy.

Lanzarote

Bazar Karina
✉ Avenida de las Playas (near Hotel San Antonio), Puerto del Carmen

Bazar TPV
✉ Avenida de las Playas (harbour end), Puerto del Carmen

Charlie's Bazar and Charlie's Anexo
✉ Avenida de las Playas (Arena Dorada commercial centre), Puerto del Carmen

Pedro y Nicholás Martin
✉ 2 Calle Gen Goded, Arrecife

Perfumeria Charlie
✉ Avenida de las Playas (next to casino), Puerto del Carmen

Santos
✉ Avenida el Jablillo, Costa Teguise

Zodiac Electronics
✉ Avenida de las Playas (Columbus commercial centre, Puerto del Carmen

Fuerteventura
Bazar Insular
✉ Calle Gen Franco, Corralejo

Bazar Korina
✉ Calle Gen Franco, Corralejo

Manrique Designs

Fundacíon César Manrique Shops
T-shirts and other clothes with Manrique logos and designs, jewellery and other goods to his design, and prints of his work.
✉ **Main shop: Taro de Tahíche**
Other shops: 26 José Betancort, Arrecife
10 Diaz Otilía, Arrecife; La Lonja, Teguise
47 Avenida de las Playas, Puerto del Carmen

Crafts
Most typical of the island crafts are fine weaving, embroidery and lacework, seen in high-quality tablecoths, placemats, bed-spreads and handkerchiefs. You'll also see good costume jewellery (often including peridot, the translucent semi-precious volcanic stone), basketware, straw hats, and unusual local pottery, traditionally made without a potters' wheel. Delicate woodwork includes *timples*, the tiny Canarian stringed instrument that originated at Teguise.

Artesanía de Haría
✉ 4 Calle Barranco, Haría, Lanzarote ⏰ Tue–Fri 10–1, Mon & Sat 10–1, 4–6:30

Artesanía Lanzaroteña
✉ Plaza 18 de Julio, Teguise
⏰ Closed Sat

Casa Marcos
Handicrafts and ceramics
✉ Villaverde, Fuerteventura
☎ 928 86 82 85

Lace and Embroidery Workshops
✉ Lajares, Fuerteventura

English Bookshop
If you need a blockbuster for the beach or history of the island, visit Bookswop I and Bookswop II, English bookshops in Puerto del Carmen. You'll find them at the Centro Costa Luz, opposite the San Antonio Hotel, Avenida de las Playas, and on the corner of Calle Timanfaya at the other end of the Avenida. As well as new and secondhand books, they have a wide range of English-language magazines.

Edible Souvenirs
Consumables that make interesting presents or tasty reminders of your stay include *mojo* sauces (▶ 82), available in small gift packs, and local wine, which can be chosen and sampled in the *bodegas* of Lanzarote's Geria Valley (▶ 26).

Children's Activities

Children Welcome
The islanders, like other Spaniards, never make kids feel excluded. It's a sign, perhaps, of their affection for children, that restaurants, bars and cafés don't generally list children's menus and children's portions. Instead, children are warmly welcomed, indulged, given little portions, and allowed in to any establishment at any hour of day or night.

Lanzarote and Fuerteventura – especially the latter – don't offer many attractions created especially with children in mind; what they *do* have, however, is the most wonderful beaches in Europe. Some of the best choices for families with children are given below.

Beaches for Families

Lanzarote

Caleton Blanca
Warm and sheltered. The swimming is safe here and there are rock pools to explore.
✉ 1km south of Orzola

Papagayo
Four connected beaches considered to be the best on the island (▶ 50–1).
✉ 6km east of Playa Blanca

Playa Grande
A good base for watersports (▶ 65).
✉ Puerto del Carmen

Fuerteventura

Corralejo Dunes
Superb dunes within reach of civilisation (▶ 18).
✉ Corralejo

Sotavento Beach
Long expanse of glorious sand. More sheltered than many beaches on this windy island (▶ 85).
✉ Jandía Peninsula

Other Attractions

Many of the sights thrill kids every bit as much as grown-ups. The sights most likely to appeal to the younger generation are listed here.

Lanzarote

Arrieta

Cueva de los Verdes
The haunting music and lighting combine to make a visit to this fascinating cave system a magical experience for children (▶ 17).
☎ 928 17 32 20 🕐 Regular tours daily 10–5

Jameos del Agua
Spotting the tiny blind white crabs, the amazing auditorium in a cave, and – most of all – the Casa de los Volcanes hands-on science museum at the top of the cliff will fascinate and amuse any child (▶ 22).
☎ 928 84 80 20 🕐 Daily 9:30–6:45; Tue, Fri, Sat open till 3AM

Costa Teguise
Ocean Park
This water park has fantastic, colourful waterslides and flumes, lovely heated swimming pools and sunloungers and shaded areas for the grown-ups. Kids aged 2–12 pay half price, over 12s full price.
✉ 2km inland from Costa Teguise ☎ 928 59 21 28 🕐 Daily 10–6 (10–5 in winter)

Guatiza
Jardín de Cactus
Is that cactus real? Especially the giant cactus outside? Go and see. One thing is for certain, the 1,400 varieties inside the garden are definitely genuine and very weird (▶ 23).

Guinate
Parque Tropical
Little ones will enjoy this bird world in northern Lanzarote, where some 300 species of

birds can be seen (➤ 62) and there are regular shows by performing parrots.

☎ 928 83 55 00 🕐 Daily 10–5

Puerto del Carmen
Blue Delfin
Variety of trips and mini-cruises daily, plus free bus transfers.

☎ 928 51 23 23

Submarine Safaris
Journey in a real submarine, with high-tech viewing options.

✉ Puerto Calero ☎ 928 51 28 98

San Bartolomé
Eurokart
Lanzarote's go-karting track. Karts come in all sizes to suit adults as well as children. The site also has a bar, cafeteria and playground. A fun family outing.

✉ On Arrecife road ☎ 928 51 21 95

Taro de Tahíche
Fundación César Manrique
Children will be entranced by the house Manrique made for himself, especially the underground rooms in spherical lava bubbles (➤ 19). The adults will be fascinated too.

Manrique Mobiles
Manrique's mischievous, childlike inventiveness strikes a chord with the youngest art-lovers when they see his mad mobiles, standing at junctions and roundabouts like giant coloured toys turning, whirling and whizzing in the wind. See if you can spot the one at the airport as soon as you arrive in Lanzarote.

Timanfaya
Islote de Hilario
Only the youngest or weariest of children could fail to be astonished by the fire and water magic at the hottest spot on the volcanic island (➤ 20–1).

Yaiza
Camel Rides
Not for everyone, but unlike with other camel rides, on these you don't sit on the camel but in seats on the animal's side. Rides are based at the Camel Park north of Yaiza (➤ 58).

Fuerteventura

Corralejo
Carnival
A dazzling show which allows wild behaviour. Failing that, enjoy the crazy noise, colour and flamboyance of any local fiesta.

🕐 Feb or Mar

Catamarán Celia Cruz
Boat trips to Lobos Island and Corralejo beaches.

☎ 616 99 22 43 🕐 Mon, Tue, Wed, 12AM–1:30PM

Lajita
Zoo Safari de Camellos
The main attraction of this small zoo park is a 30-minute ride on one of its herd of 250 dromedaries. Ponies and donkeys are also available for rides. Toucans, cranes, parrots, pelicans and ostriches are the most spectacular of its 200 species of birds and there are also lizards and crocodiles. You can buy exotic flora at its garden centre.

☎ 928 16 11 35 🕐 Daily 9–7

Late Nights
Your children will be quick to notice one Spanish custom they'll want to follow on holiday: there is no bedtime. Spanish families can often be seen out as late as midnight, having dinner or going for a stroll together. Restaurants think nothing of catering for children in the evening. Even at home, children are often up playing while the grown-ups talk until late. It's taken for granted that children are a constant part of family life.

Sports – on Water

Wind (for Windsurfers)
It is the regular, strong north-by-northwest trade wind (known as Los Alisios and often reaching force 4 or 5) blowing in from the Atlantic that makes Lanzarote and Fuerteventura such an excellent centre for windsurfing. The winds don't always blow, however: the average reliability rate is around 50 per cent in winter and 60–75 per cent in summer. The western, windward coasts can offer thrilling sport for experienced windsurfers, but beware – El Cotillo beach on Fuerteventura is said to break more kit than any other surf location in Europe!

Big Game Fishing
Hunting for shark, barracuda, swordfish, marlin, tuna, wahoo, dorado and the other big Atlantic fish is popular on both islands. Hire a boat or join an excursion.

Lanzarote

Puerto Calero
Catlanza
Daily deep sea fishing excursions by catamaran. Yachts and motorboats for private hire.
✉ **Puerto Calero** ☎ 928 51 30 22

Fuerteventura

Corrajelo
Barvik
Hunting for shark, marlin, tuna, wahoo, dorado and other big Atlantic fish.
✉ **Muelle Deportivo** ☎ 928 17 51 55

Pez Velero
Daily excursions in 33ft catamaran fishing for barracuda, tuna, bluefish and bass.
✉ **Muelle Deportivo** ☎ 928 86 61 73

Siña Maria I
✉ **Muelle Deportivo** ☎ 928 86 70 00

Diving & Scuba Diving
The good underwater visibility of the Atlantic ocean, in a climate zone where diving is possible all year round, has made this a favourite sport on the two islands. The underwater lava has created many reefs, caves and unusual rock formations. There is an abundance of wildlife to be seen, including sharks, eels, octopus and rays, as well as big fish, sponges, anemones, crustaceans and and colourful growths of coral.

Lanzarote

Costa Teguise
Calipso Diving
International courses in diving and scuba diving.
✉ **Centro Commercial Nautical, Avenida de los Islas Canarias** ☎ 928 59 08 79

Diving Lanzarote
High-quality scuba diving centre on Las Cucharas Beach, with variety of hire and excursion options, including night diving.
✉ **104 Apartado de Correos, Costa Teguise** ☎ 928 59 04 07

Puerto del Carmen
Atlantic Diving Center
Diving courses from the main beach.
✉ **Aparthotel Fariones Playa, 2 Calle Acatife** ☎ 928 51 02 00

RC Diving
Try-out lessons, training courses, organised dives. Prices include all equipment.
✉ **38 Avenida de las Playas** ☎ 928 00 34 28

Safari Diving
This PADI five-star, highly professional centre for diving includes instruction and welcomes divers of all qualifications, as well as disabled divers, beginners, non-divers, and children, for a wide range of courses lasting from 4 hours to 21 days. Organised dives include night diving. Prices include all equipment.
✉ **Playa Chica (near the port)** ☎ 928 51 04 96

Fuerteventura

Corralejo
Dive Center Corralejo
Enjoy a whole day's dive with instructor, including audio-visual training. If you are an experienced diver with certification and logbook, the Dive Center offers boat dives daily (except Sun) from 8:30AM–1:30PM, including two dives in different locations.
✉ **29 Apartado de Correos**
☎ **928 86 62 43**

Surfing
Fantastic wind and waves make these islands great for surfers.

Lanzarote

La Santa
La Santa Surf
This is *not* part of La Santa Sport complex. Take a surfing safari – this includes transport, lunch, equipment hire and instruction. Equipment rental only also possible.
✉ **La Santa** ☎ **928 84 02 79**

Fuerteventura

Corralejo
Ineika Funcenter Surfschool
A range of courses from one to 14 days, fully inclusive of equipment, transfers and video training. Other equipment, such as boards and wetsuits, available for rent.
✉ **53 Ineika Apts** ☎ **928 53 57 44**

Natural Surf
Instruction courses and equipment hire.
✉ **Calle Palangre** ☎ **928 86 73 07**

Ventura Surf
Instruction courses and equipment hire
✉ **Maya de la Galera** ☎ **928 86 62 95**

Windsurfing
This is by far the most popular sport in the Canary Islands. Every main resort beach in Lanzarote and Fuerteventura has facilities for windsurfing rentals and instruction. Fuerteventura is considered one of the world's best locations for windsurfing, and Jandía's Playa de Sotavento is the site of the annual World Windsurfing Championships mid-July to mid-August.

Lanzarote

Costa Teguise
Surf Club Celeste
Courses and equipment hire at Playa de las Cucharas by the hour or day.
✉ **Centro Commercial las Maretas** ☎ **928 59 08 79**

Fuerteventura

Corralejo
Flag Beach Windsurf Center
✉ **Grandes Playas** ☎ **928 53 55 39**

Ventura Surf
Tuition and rentals from one hour to 14 days.
✉ **8 Hoplaco Aptos** ☎ **928 86 62 95**

Playa Barca
Center René Egli
The Jandía peninsula's principal windsurfing base, with tuition and rentals, right on Sotavento beach.
✉ **Sol Hotel Los Gorriones**
☎ **928 54 74 83**

Wind (for Holidaymakers)
The north-by-northwest trade wind brings stable, rain-free days with some cloud. On the north or west of the islands, the wind can be troublesome, and the cloud cover excessive. In the south and east, it means pefect holiday weather. The occasional alternatives are the moist southerly winds or the unpleasant, warm dry sirocco that blows sand over from the Sahara.

Sports – on Land

Grin and Bare It
Topless sunbathing is acceptable on all beaches, especially the main beaches of Puerto del Carmen, Costa Teguise, Playa Blanca, Corralejo and Jandía. Naturism, or stripping off completely, is not acceptable on resort beaches, but common on any secluded stretch of coast, or beaches outside resorts, such as Playa Papagayo on Lanzarote, or, on Fuerteventura, the Corralejo beach away from the hotels.

Aerial Sports

Lanzarote

Aviador Flying School
Excursions and lessons, based at the airport.
☎ 928 35 41 93

Lanzarote Skydive Centre
Parachute jumps.
☎ 928 84 01 14

Cycling
Thanks to the dry weather and lack of traffic, cycle touring is fun on these islands. Choose between easy-going flatter terrain near the resorts, and more challenging hills in the interior. Wherever you go, remember to take plenty of drinking water.

Lanzarote

Costa Teguise
Hot Bike
Bike hire by week, day or half-day; maps, baby seats, etc also available. The company also organises bike-and-jeep outings, for example to the Famara Cliffs.
✉ Near Playa de las Cucharas
☎ 928 59 03 04

Tommy's Bikes
The leading and longest established hire shop for top-quality touring, racing and mountain bikes. This friendly, helpful company gives free advice and maps, and recommends and organises island tours and excursions. A typical excursion lasts a whole day, including jeep transfers, bikes, water, tour guide, boat transfers where necessary.
✉ 14 Apartado de Correos,

Calle de la Galeta, Galeon Playa (near Playa del Jablillo)
☎ 928 59 23 27

Fuerteventura

Corralejo
Vulcano Biking
Touring cycles and mountain bikes for hire.
✉ 10 Calle Acorazado España
☎ 928 53 57 06

Golf

Lanzarote

Costa Teguise
Club de Golf de Costa Teguise
Lanzarote's only golf course is considered one of Europe's most unusual and exciting places to play. The tender green turf of the 18-hole, 72-par course looks dazzling amid the dark hills, cacti and palms within sight of the Atlantic. No handicap is required. The course offers a driving range, putting and pitching greens, buggy, trolley and club hire, and a charming club house with bar-restaurant, lounge and pro-shop. Lessons are also available.
✉ 2km up Avenida del Golf
☎ 928 59 05 12

Horse Riding

Lanzarote

Puerto del Carmen
Rancho Texas Equestrian Centre
Pony trekking, dressage, jumping and riding lessons available. Also self-catering accommodation for hire.
✉ Signposted from Playa de los Pocillos beach ☎ 928 17 32 47

Uga
Lanzarote a Caballo (Lanzarote on Horseback)
Full- or half-day excursions to the Geria Valley, Playa Quemada or Playa Blanca. Riding lessons also offered.
✉ **On Arrecife–Yaiza road, close to Uga** ☎ **928 83 03 14**

Fuerteventura

Corralejo
Fuerteadventure
✉ **In the development at Parques Holandés, south of Corralejo**

Motorbiking
A motorbike is a good way to explore the spectacular terrain. (▶ panel)

Lanzarote

Puerto del Carmen
Classic Drive
✉ **Avenida de las Playas, Centro Commercial Maritimo**
☎ **928 51 23 17**

Sunbike & Moto
✉ **Centro Commercial Playa Blanca** ☎ **928 51 34 40**

Fuerteventura

Corralejo
Volcano Biking
✉ **10 Calle Acorazado España**
☎ **928 53 57 06**

Sports Centres

Lanzarote

Costa Teguise
Toca Sport
Tennis and squash courts are available, plus a swimming pool, gym, sauna, table tennis – and yoga classes.
✉ **Avenida del Jablillo**
☎ **928 59 06 17**

Puerto del Carmen
Castellana Sport
Fully equipped gym and squash courts open to the public near the beach in Lanzarote's main resort. Also offers aerobics classes.
✉ **2 Calle Guanapay** ☎ **928 51 14 93**

Centro Deportivo Farioner
Large complex including a swimming pool and squash and tennis courts.
✉ **Playa Blanca, next to Los Fariones Hotel** ☎ **928 82 52 08**
🕔 **9:30AM–10PM**

Walking
There are numerous possible routes on both islands, but note that walking on the volcanic *malpaís* is difficult and uncomfortable. Don't set off on your own, and take adequate supplies (of water, high-energy food and protective gear) with you on longer trips.

Lanzarote

Timanfaya
ICONA National Parks Walking Service
Two guided walks in Timanfaya National Park (▶ 56), one a volcano walk and one along the coast. The groups are small and the emphasis is on the geology of the *malpaís* and its native species.
✉ **Mancha Blanca Visitor Centre** ☎ **928 84 08 39**

Fuerteventura

Villaverde
Hannelore von der Twer
Guided walks in many areas including Monte Arena.
✉ **Villa Volcana** ☎ **928 86 86 90 or 608 92 83 80**

Motorbiking
The open roads and lack of traffic make the islands attractive places for biking. A few words of warning, however. If you intend going offroad make sure you have a sufficiently powerful machine not to get bogged down in sand, particularly if you have a pillion rider or much luggage. Beware too that lava tracks are extremely bumpy. Fill up with petrol on Saturdays, as on Sundays many petrol stations only have automatic pumps working. The smallest note they accept is 1,000 ptas, which will buy far more fuel that you need if you only have a small petrol tank. And, finally, the cost of hiring a bike may not be any cheaper than a car – shop around as much as you can.

Gastronomy & Nightlife

The Wine-grower's Art
In 1964–5 the region around La Geria, Lanzarote's main wine-producing area, was dubbed 'Engineering without Engineers' by the Metropolitan Museum of Modern Art in New York because of its ingenious 'vineyards'. The largest *bodega* on the island, El Grifo, now exports its wines all over Europe.

Gastronomy

Lanzarote

La Geria
Bodegas Barreto
Free wine tasting at this Lanzarote wine cellar.
✉ **At El Campesino, on La Geria road** ☎ **928 52 07 17** 🕐 **Daily 10–6:30**

Mozaga
Bodegas Mozaga
Wine tasting and wine buying at this popular producer of Lanzarote wines.
✉ **On Arrecife–Tinajo road** ☎ **928 52 04 85** 🕐 **Daily 8:30AM–6PM**

San Bartolomé
El Grifo Bodega and Museo del Vino
The oldest working *bodega* on Lanzarote. Take a look at the old winepress and 18th-century wine-making equipment, have a half-hour guided stroll in the vineyards and enjoy the wine tasting. A sculpture of a griffin by César Manrique stands at the entrance to the *bodega*.
✉ **On road to Uga** ☎ **928 80 05 86** 🕐 **Bodega daily 10–4, Museo daily 10:30–6**

Uga
El Faro
Tasting of Lanzarote's salty, traditionally made goat's cheeses.
✉ **On Teguise–Uga road** ☎ **928 17 31 13**

Casinos

Lanzarote

Puerto del Carmen
Casino
Slot machines, blackjack and roulette tables, as well as restaurant, bar and entertainment. Admittance is strictly for over-18s only – and you will need your passport as proof of age.
✉ **12 Avenida de las Playas** ☎ **928 51 50 00** 🕐 **Slot machines: 11PM–4AM. Bar and game hall: 8PM–4AM. Restaurant: 9PM–2AM**

Discos and Late-night Bars
All the resorts on both islands have late-night bars with music, but there are few real discos or dance venues. Those listed here open around 9 or 10PM (although they only really start filling up around midnight) and stay open until 2 or 4AM.

Lanzarote
Avenida de las Playas in Puerto del Carmen is Lanzarote's 'entertainment mile', with a large number of late-night bars featuring live music and dancing. The focal point for most of the city's discos and nightclubs is the Centro Atlantico block, situated on the Avenida about half-way along the main beach. Of the other resorts, only Costa Teguise really offers a full choice of bars and discos which open till late.

Arrecife
La Antigua
A popular music bar.
✉ **62 Calle José Antonio**

La Naos
Five bars and dance floor in a marquee and outdoor terrace; popular with the jet set.
✉ **Puerto Naos** 🕐 **Thu–Sat 11PM–4AM**

Arrieta

Jameos del Agua
After dark on Tuesday, Friday and Saturday, the water caverns in the north of the island become a popular nightclub, where crowds drink, dine and dance nightly in the extraordinary underground setting. There is also a folklore show on these nights.

✉ **Near Arrieta, 26km north of Arrecife** ☎ **928 84 80 20** 🕐 **Tue, Fri & Sat 7PM–3AM. Folklore show 11PM**

Costa Teguise

Baobab Club
✉ **2nd floor, Centro Teguise Playa (Jablillo area)**

Puerto del Carmen

Basement Club
✉ **Downstairs, Centro Atlantico**

Dreams Disco
✉ **Downstairs, Centro Atlantico**

Harley Rock Diner and Disco
The entrance looks like a jukebox. 'Ladies' Fantasy' muscle show held every Thursday.
✉ **Upstairs, Centro Columbus**

Lips Nightclub
Striptease show for over-18s.
✉ **Centro Atlantico** ☎ **928 51 31 68** 🕐 **Daily 10PM–4AM**

Moonlight Bay
Bands and cabaret shows
✉ **Playa de los Pocillos** 🕐 **Daily 9PM–4AM**

Papagayo
✉ **Set back from street. Centro Atlantico**

Paradise
✉ **2nd floor, Centro Columbus**

Fuerteventura

Caleta de Fustes

La Polka
✉ **Caleta de Fustes**

Corralejo

The Blue Rock
Small bar playing rock and blues music
✉ **Just off the front, to the right of the tourist office**

Morro del Jable

Angels
✉ **Avenida del Saladar**

Puerto del Rosario

Taifa
✉ **2 Calle Juan Tadeo Cabrera**

Hotels
The main hotels offer simple entertainment, such as cabaret, dancing, karaoke or professional musicians, every evening from about 10PM–midnight.

There's no need to be a guest at the hotel to enjoy the entertainment. Simply check the weekly programme displayed at hotels and make your choice.

Lanzarote

Costa Teguise
Melía Salinas Hotel
✉ **Avenida Islas Canarias**

Playa Blanca
Timanfaya Palace Hotel
✉ **West of the harbour**

Puerto del Carmen
Los Fariones Hotel
✉ **Harbour end of main beach**

Fuerteventura

Corralejo
Riu Palace Tres Islas
✉ **Playas de Corralejo**

Canarian Wrestling
A favourite spectator sport for the islanders is their traditional wrestling (*Lucha Canaria*), for which the combatants wear a particular style of shorts and shirt. Wrestlers work in teams, whose members are pitted against each other one-to-one, in turns. The fight involves holding onto the side of your opponent's shorts and attempting to throw him to the ground. It's slow and cautious, with long waits for sudden moves. Contests are staged from time to time, and your hotel or the tourist office should have details of forthcoming matches. This 'clean' sport is very fair and totally different from European wrestling. It provides great family entertainment. Tourists are made welcome, and this is a good way to meet the locals.

What's On When

Carnival Islands

Carnaval brings two weeks of music, dancing, noise, parades, craziness and energy, which on Lanzarote is held mainly on the waterside promenades of Arrecife and Puerto del Carmen. It ends on Ash Wednesday with the zany ceremony of the Burial of the Sardine. For this farcical finale, black-clad mourners sob as a tiny coffin containing the sardine is buried on the seashore. The festival may be less grandiose on Fuerteventura, but has the advantage of being held at several places all over the island. Small towns and villages will put on their own days of colourful, enthusiastic parades and processions, including a day devoted to the Childrens' Carnival.

January

Cabalgata de los Reyes Magos Festival (Three Kings Parade, 5 Jan): Teguise.

February

Fiesta de Nuestra Señora de Candelaria (Candlemas, 2 Feb): A big festival and pilgrimage in certain villages, for example Gran Tarajal and La Oliva on Fuerteventura. *Carnaval* (two weeks, dates vary each year): Especially exuberant in Arrecife on Lanzarote, and Corralejo on Fuerteventura (► panel).

March/April

Easter: look out for big events all over the islands during Easter Week.

May

Fiestas on Fuerteventura include:
Tarajalejo (8 May)
La Lajita (13 May).

June

Fiesta de San Juan (24 Jun): celebrating the midsummer, Haria, Lanzarote.
Corpus Christi: Arrecife, Lanzarote. Patterns of coloured sand are used to decorate the ground.

July

Fiesta de Nuestra Señora de Regla (2 Jul): Pajara, Fuerteventura.
Fiesta de San Buenaventura (14 Jul): Betancuria, Fuerteventura, festival to honour the town's patron saint and the incorporation of the island into Spain.
Fiesta de Nuestra Señora del Carmen (16 Jul): Teguise, Lanzarote; Corralejo, Morro del Jable, Fuerteventura.
Fiesta (last Sat in Jul) La Pared, Fuerteventura.

August

Fiestas de Carmen (two weeks from 1 Aug): Puerto del Carmen, Lanzarote. On the last Saturday fishing boats put out to sea with charmingly decorated effigies of the saint aboard.
Fiesta de San Ginés (whole month): everywhere, but especially Arrecife, Lanzarote. Processions, parades and traditional dancing in the streets.
Semana de la Juventud (Youth Week, second week): Gran Tarajal, Fuerteventura.

September

Fiesta de Nuestra Señora de Antigua (8 Sep): in honour of Antigua's patron saint, Fuerteventura.
Fiesta de Nuestra Señora de Guadalupe (8 Sep): Teguise, Lanzarote .
Virgen de los Volcanes (15 Sep): general pilgrimage (*romería*) to Mancha Blanca, Lanzarote. The highlight is a re-enactment of the Virgin stopping the lava flow.
Fiesta de Nuestra Señora de la Peña (3rd Sat): Vega del Rio de Palma, Fuerteventura.
Fiesta (29 Sep): Tuineje, Fuerteventura.

October

Fiesta de Nuestra Señora del Rosario (7 Oct): Puerto del Rosario, Fuerteventura.
Battle of Tamacita (13 Oct): Tuineje, Fuerteventura.

November

Fiesta de San Diego de Alcalá (13 Nov): Gran Tarajal, Fuerteventura.

December

Christmas: nativity plays and processions take place all over the islands.

Practical Matters

Above: *the road to Sóo, Lanzarote*
Right: *shell sculpture in the harbour at Puerto del Rosario, Fuerteventura*

TIME DIFFERENCES

GMT	Canaries	Germany	USA (NY)	Netherlands	Spain
12 noon	12 noon →	1PM →	7AM ←	1PM →	1PM →

BEFORE YOU GO

WHAT YOU NEED

- ● Required
- ○ Suggested
- ▲ Not required

	UK	Germany	USA	Netherlands	Spain
Passport/National Identity Card	●	●	●	●	●
Visa	▲	▲	▲	▲	▲
Onward or return ticket	▲	▲	○	▲	▲
Health inoculations	▲	▲	▲	▲	▲
Travel insurance	○	○	○	○	○
Driving licence (national or international; Spain national only)	●	●	●	●	●
Health insurance	○	○	●	○	○
Health documentation	▲	▲	▲	▲	▲

WHEN TO GO

Lanzarote/Fuerteventura

High season

Low season

JAN	FEB	MAR	APR	MAY	JUN	JUL	AUG	SEP	OCT	NOV	DEC
21°C	21°C	23°C	24°C	25°C	26°C	28°C	29°C	29°C	27°C	24°C	21°C

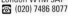

☀ Sun

⛅ Sunshine & showers

TOURIST OFFICES

In the UK
Spanish National Tourist Office
23 Manchester Square
London W1M 5AP
☎ (020) 7486 8077

In the USA
Spanish National Tourist Office
666 Fifth Ave, 35th floor
New York, NY 10103
☎ (212) 265-8822

Other SNTOs in Chicago,

Los Angeles, Miami
In Canada
Spanish National Tourist Office
102 Bloor St W, 34th floor
Toronto, Ontario
M4W 3E2
☎ (416) 961-3131

118

POLICE 091

FIRE 091

AMBULANCE 091

WHEN YOU ARE THERE

ARRIVING

At Lanzarote All flights arrive at Arrecife airport (☎ 928 81 14 50), which lies between Arrecife and its main resort, Puerto del Carmen.

At Fuerteventura All flights arrive at Puerto del Rosario's small airport (☎ 928 85 12 50), which lies between the island's capital and Caleta de Fustes.

Arrecife Airport To Puerto del Carmen	Journey times	
	🚂	20 minutes
10 kilometres	🚌	N/A
	🚗	10 minutes

Puerto del Rosario Airport To Corralejo	Journey times	
	🚂	1 hour
35 kilometres	🚌	N/A
	🚗	45 minutes

MONEY

Lanzarote and Fuerteventura use the Spanish peseta (pta). Banknotes come in denominations of 1,000, 2,000, 5,000 and 10,000 ptas. As well as the one peseta coin, which has almost negligible value, coins are valued at 5, 10, 25, 50, 100, 200 and 500 ptas. The Canary Islands' free trade status has kept them from joining the European single currency for the time being.

TIME

Lanzarote and Fuerteventura (and all the Canaries) follow Greenwich Mean Time (GMT), but from late March – when clocks are put forward one hour – until late September, summer time operates (GMT+1).

CUSTOMS

YES

As the Canaries are a free-trade zone there are no restrictions at all on the amounts of alcohol, tobacco, perfume and other goods that can be brought into the islands. It would be pointless to take most goods into these islands in the expectation of saving money, however: almost everything is cheaper in the Canaries than it is at home. Visitors may bring an unlimited amount of Spanish or foreign currency but should declare any amount exceeding a million pesetas to avoid difficulties on leaving.

NO

There are a few obvious exceptions to the above, notably drugs, firearms, obscene material and unlicensed animals.

CONSULATES

UK
Las Palmas, Gran
Canaria
☎ 928 26 25 08

Germany
Las Palmas, Gran
Canaria
☎ 928 27 57 00

USA
Las Palmas, Gran
Canaria
☎ 928 27 12 59

Netherlands
Las Palmas, Gran
Canaria
☎ 928 24 23 82

WHEN YOU ARE THERE

TOURIST OFFICES

In Lanzarote

● Head office:
Cabilda Insular de
Lanzarote
Consejería de Turismo
Patronato de Turismo
Blas Cabrera Felipe
35500 Arrecife
☎ 928 81 17 62
Fax: 928 80 00 80

● Local offices:
Arrecife: Parque Municipal
☎ 928 81 18 60
Puerto del Carmen: in a
distinctive octagonal
beachside chalet beside
the main beach, on Avenida
de las Playas
☎ 928 51 53 37
Playa Blanca: at the ferry
harbour

In Fuerteventura

● Head office:
Patronato de Turismo de
Fuerteventura
Avenida Constitución 5
Puerto del Rosario
☎ 928 53 08 44
Fax: 928 85 16 95

● Local offices:
Puerto del Rosario airport
☎ 928 86 06 04
Corralejo: Plaza Pública
☎ 928 86 62 35
C C Castillo Cenro, Caleta
de Fustes
☎ 928 16 32 86
Morro Jable: in the
shopping centre, Jandía
Beach
☎ 928 54 07 76

NATIONAL HOLIDAYS

J	F	M	A	M	J	J	A	S	O	N	D
2	1	1(1)	(1)	2	1	1	1		1	1	3

1 January	Año Nuevo (New Year's Day)
6 January	Los Reyes (Epiphany)
2 February	La Candelaria (Candlemas)
19 March	San José (St Joseph's Day)
March/April	Pascua (Easter) Thu, Fri, Sun of Easter Week, and following Mon
1 May	Dia del Trabajo (Labour Day)
May/June	Corpus Christi
25 July	Santiago (St James's Day)
15 August	Asunción (Assumption)
12 October	Hispanidad (Columbus Day)
1 November	Todos los Santos (All Saints' Day)
6 December	Constitucion (Constitution Day)
8 December	Immaculada Concepción (Immaculate Conception)
25 December	Navidad (Christmas)

OPENING HOURS

○ Shops   ● Post Offices
● Offices   ◐ Museums/Monuments
● Banks   ◐ Pharmacies

| 8AM | 9AM | 10AM | NOON | 1PM | 2PM | 4PM | 5PM | 7PM |

□ Day   □ Midday
□ Evening

In resorts, some shops keep longer hours and may
also be open on Sunday. Chemists keep similar hours
to other shops but are usually closed on Saturday
afternoons. At least one chemist per town is normally
open after hours. Many bars open for breakfast
around 7AM and stay open till about 1AM or later the
following morning. Even outside these hours you can
often find a bar open. Expect bars to be closed from
about 3AM–6AM. Museum opening times can be
unpredictable – many open in the mornings only.

DRIVE ON THE RIGHT

TOILETS CHARGE

PUBLIC TRANSPORT

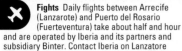

Fights Daily flights between Arrecife (Lanzarote) and Puerto del Rosario (Fuerteventura) take about half and hour and are operated by Iberia and its partners and subsidiary Binter. Contact Iberia on Lanzatore (☎ 928 84 61 01) and on Fuerteventura (☎ 928 86 05 10).

Buses Public transport on the islands is mainly confined to a slow rural bus network designed to get villagers to and from the capital (Arrecife in Lanzarote, Puerto del Rosario in Fuerteventura). Timings are for the convenience of locals rather than visitors. Buses are always called by their local colloquial name, *guaguas* (pronounced wahwahs). Main bus station at Arrecife, Lanzarote: ☎ 928 81 14 56; main bus station at Puerto del Rosario, Fuerteventura: ☎ 928 85 21 66.

Ferries Between Lanzarote and Fuerteventura (and also to other Canary Islands) ferries are run by:
Transmediterránea (in Arrecife, Lanzarote ☎ 928 81 11 88; in Puerto del Rosario, Fuerteventura ☎ 928 85 08 77)
Betancuria (in Arrecife, Lanzarote ☎ 928 81 25 34; in Corralejo, Fuerteventura ☎ 928 41 72 14)
Fred Olsen (at Playa Blanca, Lanzarote ☎ 928 51 72 66; ticket office also at harbour in Corralejo, Fuerteventura ☎ 928 53 50 90)
Armas (in Playa Blanca, Lanzarote ☎ 928 51 79 12; 90 calle Jose Antonio, Arrecife ☎ 928 82 49 31; the harbour at Corralejo, Fuerteventura ☎ 928 86 70 80).
To Isla de Lobos: Ferry Majorero from Corralejo harbour, Fuerteventura
To Isla Graciosa: Ferry from Orzola harbour, Lanzarote

CAR RENTAL

Car hire is relatively cheap on Lanzarote, but dearer on Fuerteventura. Small local firms are efficient, though the (pricier) international firms are also represented. Minor roads on both islands are often little more than dirt tracks and signposting is sporadic.

TAXIS

Cabs have a green 'for hire' light inside the windscreen, and a special SP licence plate ('*servicio público*'). Cabs are inexpensive (dearer on Fuerteventura than Lanzarote, though, simply because distances are longer).

DRIVING

There are no motorways on these two islands.

Speed limit on main roads: **90kph**

Speed limit in town: **60kph** unless indicated

Seat belts are compulsory for all passengers. Children under 10 (excluding babies in rear-facing baby seats) must ride in the back seats.

No on-the-road breath test is currently used, but driving under the influence of alcohol is strictly illegal, and consequences if involved in an accident will be severe, possibly including a jail term.

Fuel is sold as *Super* or *Extra* (leaded), *Sin plomo* (unleaded) and *Gasoleo* (diesel). Petrol stations are rare on both islands outside the capitals and the main resorts. Most service stations keep shop hours and don't always take credit cards.

Lanzarote is notorious for accidents. If involved in a serious accident, call the police on 091. If no one is injured, exchange details with other motorists involved. Hire cars and their drivers should all be insured by the hire company. Hire car companies should issue drivers with an emergency number to call in the event of a breakdown.

PERSONAL SAFETY

Crime is not a problem in Lanzarote and Fuerteventura. The greatest risk is theft by another tourist. Put all bags, clothes, etc, in the boot of your car where they cannot be seen, rather than on the back seat. If self-catering, lock all doors and windows before going out.

• Fire is a risk in hotels – locate the nearest fire exit to your room and ensure it is not blocked or locked.
• Do not leave possessions unattended on the beach or in cars.
• **In an emergency, call the police on 091.** Otherwise call or visit the Guardia Civil (Arrecife: ☎ 928 81 23 50; Puerto del Rosario: ☎ 928 85 09 09)

TELEPHONES

All phone numbers in Spain, including the Canary Islands, have 9 digits, and you must dial the whole number. To use a public payphone, you'll usually need *una tarjeta de telefóno*, a phone card. These are

widely available from tobacconists and similar shops. To dial abroad first dial 00, wait for a change of tone, then dial the international code of the country you are calling (see below).

International dialling codes	
From the Canary Islands to:	
UK:	**44**
Germany:	**49**
USA & Canada:	**1**
Netherlands:	**31**
Mainland Spain:	**9-digit number only**

POST

Post boxes are yellow, and often have a slot marked 'Extranjeros' for mail to foreign countries.
Letters or cards to the UK cost 70 ptas (up to 20g)
Postcards/letters to the US/Canada cost 120 ptas (up to 15g)
Letters within Spain cost 35 ptas. Post offices are open Mon–Fri 9–2, Sat 9–1.

ELECTRICITY

The voltage is 220/240v throughout both islands. Sockets take the standard

European two-round-pin plugs. Bring an adaptor for British or American appliances you wish to use with their usual plugs, and Americans should change the voltage setting on appliances.

TIPS/GRATUITIES

Yes ✓ No ✗		
Restaurants (service included)	✗	
Café/bar	✓	to nearest 100 ptas
Taxi	✓	10%
Porter	✓	50–100 ptas
Ushers/Usherettes	✓	25–50 ptas
Hairdressers	✓	50–300 ptas
Cloakroom/washroom attn.	✓	10–25 ptas
Tour guide	✓	200–300 ptas
Room service	✓	50–100 ptas

What To Photograph: Lanzarote's volcanic terrain, either as landscapes or in close up, provides extraordinary images of 'landscape as art'. Contrasts of black lava with dazzling white cottages are typical. Crops growing in black *picón* startle the eye. On Fuerteventura, immense dunescapes and beaches framed by sky and sea look like modern painting.
Light: be aware of the intensity of light – photographing in the early morning or evening may give the best results.
Film: most popular brands are readily available at the resorts.

HEALTH

Insurance
It is essential to have good medical health cover in case of a medical emergency, although EU nationals receive free medical treatment with the relevant documentation (form E111 for UK nationals). You may need to give a photocopy of the E111 to the doctor. German- and English-speaking doctors practise at Clinic Dr Mager, 37 Avenida de las Playas, Puerto del Carmen ☎ 928 51 26 11. There are also branches in Costa Teguise and Playa Blanca.

Dental Services
Emergency treatment may be expensive but is covered by most medical insurance (but not by form E111). Keep the bills for insurance claims.

Sun Advice
The biggest danger to health here is an incautious enjoyment of the sunshine. Not only are these islands most popular with North Europeans during the winter months when they are least accustomed to sun, but it is vital to remember that Lanzarote and Fuerteventura are 700 miles nearer the Equator than southern Spain, on the same latitude as the Sahara. Use generous amounts of sun cream, choosing a higher factor than normal, at least until your skin has begun to tan. A wide-brim hat and a T-shirt (even when swimming) are advisable for children.

Medication
Any essential medicines should be taken with you to Lanzarote or Fuerteventura. Most well-known proprietory brands of analgesics and popular remedies etc are available at all pharmacies. All medicines must be paid for, even if prescribed by a doctor.

Safe water
Tap water is safe all over the islands, except where signs indicate that water is not drinkable. However most water is desalinated and tastes unpleasant. Drink bottled water (*agua mineral*), sold either *sin gaz* (still) or *con gaz* (carbonated).

YOUTH CONCESSIONS

Lanzarote and Fuerteventura do not attract backpacking youngsters the way other holiday islands do. There are no youth hostels and few, if any, youth concessions available.

CLOTHING SIZES

Canary Islands	UK	Europe	USA	
46	36	46	36	
48	38	48	38	
50	40	50	40	Suits
52	42	52	42	
54	44	54	44	
56	46	56	46	
41	7	41	8	
42	7.5	42	8.5	
43	8.5	43	9.5	Shoes
44	9.5	44	10.5	
45	10.5	45	11.5	
46	11	46	12	
37	14.5	37	14.5	
38	15	38	15	
39/40	15.5	39/40	15.5	Shirts
41	16	41	16	
42	16.5	42	16.5	
43	17	43	17	
36	8	34	6	
38	10	36	8	
40	12	38	10	Dresses
42	14	40	12	
44	16	42	14	
46	18	44	16	
38	4.5	38	6	
38	5	38	6.5	
39	5.5	39	7	Shoes
39	6	39	7.5	
40	6.5	40	8	
41	7	41	8.5	

WHEN DEPARTING

- Always reconfirm your return flight with the airline or holiday rep at least one day before departing.
- Check in at least 2 hours before flight departure.
- Allow time to return your hire car.

LANGUAGE

People working in the tourist industry, including waiters, generally know some English. In places where few tourists venture, including bars and restaurants in Arrecife, it is helpful to know some basic Spanish.

Pronunciation guide: *b* almost like a *v*; *c* before *e* or *i* sounds like *th* otherwise like *k*; *d* can be like English *d* or like a *th*; *g* before *e* or *i* is a guttural *h*, between vowels like *h*, otherwise like *g*; *h* always silent; *j* guttural *h*; *ll* like English *lli* (as in 'million'); *ñ* sounds like *ni* in 'onion'; *qu* sound like *k*; *v* sounds a little like *b*; *z* like English *th*.

hotel	*hotel*	breakfast	*el desayuno*
room	*una habitación*	bathroom	*el cuarto de baño*
single/double/	*individual/doble/*	shower	*la ducha*
twin	*con dos camas*	balcony	*el balcón*
one/two nights	*una noche / dos*	reception	*la recepción*
	noches	key	*la llave*
reservation	*una reserva*	room service	*el servicio de*
rate	*la tarifa*		*habitaciones*

bureau de change	*cambio*	pounds sterling	*la libra esterlina*
post office	*correos*	US dollars	*dólares*
cash machine/	*cajero*	banknote	*un billete de*
ATM	*automático*		*banco*
foreign	*cambio (de*	travellers'	*cheques*
exchange	*divisas)*	cheques	*de viaje*
foreign currency	*cambio*	credit card	*la tarjeta de*
			crédito

restaurant	*restaurante*	cheers!	*salud!*
cafe-bar	*bar*	dessert	*el postre*
table	*una mesa*	water	*agua*
menu	*la carta*	(house) wine	*vino (de la casa)*
set menus	*platos*	beer	*cerveza*
	combinados	drink	*la bebida*
today's set menu	*el plato del día*	bill	*la cuentra*
wine list	*la carta de vinos*	the toilet	*los servicios*

plane	*el avion*	single/return...	*de ida / ...de ida y*
airport	*el aeropuerto*		*vuelta*
bus	*el autobús*	ticket office	*el despacho de*
	('guagua')		*billetes*
ferry	*el ferry*	timetable	*el horario*
terminal	*terminus*	seat	*un asiento*
ticket	*un billete*	reserved seat	*un asiento*
			reservado

yes	*si*	is there..?, do you	*hay...?*
no	*no*	have..?	
please	*por favor*	I don't speak	*No hablo*
thank you	*gracias*	Spanish	*español*
hello/hi	*hola!*	I am ...	*Soy ...*
hello/good day	*buenos dias*	I have ..	*Tengo ...*
sorry, pardon me	*perdon*	help!	*socorro!*
bye, see you	*hasta luego*	how much	*cuánto es?*
that's fine	*está bien*	open	*abierto*
what?	*como?*	closed	*cerrado*

INDEX

Acknowledgements
The Automobile Assocation wishes to thank the following photographers, libraries and associations for their assistance in the preparation of this book:

MARY EVANS PICTURE LIBRARY 10
MRI BANKERS' GUIDE TO FOREIGN CURRENCY 119
MUSEO DE HISTORIA DE TENERIFE 11
NATURE PHOTOGRAPHERS LTD 86b (Brinsley Burbidge)
PICTURES COLOUR LIBRARY F/cover (woman in traditional costume)

The remaining photographs are held in the Association's own photo library (**AA PHOTO LIBRARY**) and were taken by Steve Day, with the exception of the following: F/cover (El Golfo, windsurfers), B/cover (wine barrels) and pages 7b, 7c, 15b, 16b, 17b, 23b, 24b, 36/7, 41b, 47b, 50/1, 55b, 64, 65, 66/7, 68b, 69a, 69b, 71b, 73b, 82b, 83a, which were taken by Clive Sawyer.

Copy editor: Hilary Hughes   Page layout: Jo Tapper
Revision management: Outcrop Publishing Services, Cumbria

Dear Essential Traveller

Your comments, opinions and recommendations are very important to us. So please help us to improve our travel guides by taking a few minutes to complete this simple questionnaire.

You do not need a stamp (unless posted outside the UK). If you do not want to cut this page from your guide, then photocopy it or write your answers on a plain sheet of paper.

Send to: **The Editor, AA World Travel Guides, FREEPOST SCE 4598, Basingstoke RG21 4GY.**

Your recommendations...

We always encourage readers' recommendations for restaurants, nightlife or shopping – if your recommendation is used in the next edition of the guide, we will send you a *FREE* AA *Essential* Guide of your choice. Please state below the establishment name, location and your reasons for recommending it.

_____

_____

_____

_____

Please send me **AA *Essential*** _____

(*see list of titles inside the front cover*)

About this guide...

Which title did you buy?

AA *Essential* _____

Where did you buy it? _____

When? m m / y y

Why did you choose an AA *Essential* Guide? _____

_____

_____

_____

_____

Did this guide meet your expectations?

Exceeded ☐   Met all ☐   Met most ☐   Fell below ☐

Please give your reasons _____

_____

_____

_____

continued on next page...

Were there any aspects of this guide that you particularly liked? _____

_____

_____

_____

Is there anything we could have done better? _____

_____

_____

_____

_____

About you...

Name (*Mr/Mrs/Ms*) _____

    Address _____

_____

_____ Postcode _____

    Daytime tel nos _____

Which age group are you in?
    Under 25 ☐ 25–34 ☐ 35–44 ☐ 45–54 ☐ 55–64 ☐ 65+ ☐

How many trips do you make a year?
    Less than one ☐ One ☐ Two ☐ Three or more ☐

Are you an AA member? Yes ☐ No ☐

About your trip...

When did you book? m m / y y   When did you travel? m m / y y
How long did you stay? _____
Was it for business or leisure? _____
Did you buy any other travel guides for your trip?
    If yes, which ones? _____

_____

Thank you for taking the time to complete this questionnaire. Please send
    it to us as soon as possible, and remember, you do not need a stamp
    (*unless posted outside the UK*).

Happy Holidays!